ASSESSMENT MASTERS

Includes Mid-Unit and End-of-Unit Assessments

D1319348

PROGRAM AUTHOR

Timothy Shanahan, Ph.D.

Professor of Urban Education at the University of Illinois at Chicago

Director of the UIC Center for Literacy

GLOBE FEARON

Pearson Learning Group

PROJECT STAFF

Art and Design: Tricia Battipede, Evelyn Bauer, Sharon Bozek, Alison O'Brien

Editorial: Emily Shenk, Shirley White

Inventory: Jean Wohlgemuth

Marketing: Ken Clinton, Andrea Spaeth

Production/Manufacturing: Alia Lesser

Publishing Operations: Kate Matracia, Debi Schlott

ISBN: 0-13-024870-3

Printed in the United States of America

1 2 3 4 5 6 7 8 9 10   08 07 06 05

Pearson Learning Group

1-800-321-3106
www.pearsonlearning.com

CONTENTS

PLACEMENT, ASSESSMENT, AND EVALUATION IN THE **AMP** READING SYSTEM

Formal and informal evaluation give you the total picture.

Placement

The AMP Reading System is designed for middle school and high school students reading at the third, fourth, and fifth grade levels as well as for adults reading at those levels.

If your district uses one of the major large-scale, norm-referenced achievement tests such as

- Iowa Tests of Basic Skills (ITBS)
- Terra Nova (CAT6)
- Metropolitan Achievement Tests (MAT)
- Stanford Achievement Test
- Gates MacGinitie Reading Tests

for placement, students who score from the fifteenth to the thirty-fifth percentiles are good candidates for the AMP Reading System.

The Informal Reading Inventory (IRI) will give you an indication of how much support individual students will need.

The program is designed to accommodate a variety of reading levels in a single classroom. Students at the lowest reading levels will find the support they need in the *AMP Reading Online Library* with

- scaffolded guidance through the comprehension strategies
- support for vocabulary
- fluency modeling

Because each student will be starting at a different point as a reader, the goal of the AMP Reading System is to help all students achieve progress and gain competence and confidence as they apply the strategies they are learning and extend them into their reading in their other subject areas.

AMP Reading System	Students' Scores on Norm-Referenced Tests	Students' Lexile® Levels	Students' Scores on the Informal Reading Inventory
Level 1 for students in the sixth grade and above who are reading at a third to fourth grade level	15th–35th percentile	700s	Level 1 IRI 85–95
Level 2 for students in the seventh grade and above who are reading at a fourth to fifth grade level	15th–35th percentile	800s	Level 2 IRI 85–95
Level 3 for students in the eighth grade and above who are reading at a fifth to sixth grade level	15th–35th percentile	900s	Level 3 IRI 85–95

Continuous and Ongoing Progress Monitoring

Progress monitoring and evaluation in the AMP Reading System involve both formal assessment and students' self-evaluation of their progress.

At the beginning of the year, an Informal Reading Inventory (IRI) provides a starting point for evaluating students' needs.

At the beginning of a unit, students set goals for themselves as they preview the unit theme and instructional focus.

Students' daily oral and written responses in the Student Guide provide multiple opportunities for informal progress monitoring. The Student Guide lessons are also a source for grade reporting at whatever frequency your school or district recommends.

At the unit midpoint, students discuss and evaluate their learning so far in comprehension, vocabulary, and fluency and check their progress against their goals.

The Mid-Unit Assessment follows this important pause point and allows you to compare students' self-evaluation with their performance on the test. The insight you gain will guide your instructional decisions for both the class and individual students as you continue through the unit.

At the end of a unit, students again discuss what they have learned from their reading, their work with the unit strategy, their vocabulary study, and their fluency practice. They record how well they think they met their unit goals.

The End-of-Unit Assessment shows students' progress in vocabulary, comprehension, and fluency.

Testing

This book contains a Mid-Unit and End-of-Unit Assessment for each of the seven Student Guide units. Each of these multiple-choice tests has three sections:

VOCABULARY tests students' understanding of each vocabulary word they have studied.

COMPREHENSION provides a reading passage followed by questions that demonstrate students' understanding of both the passage and the unit comprehension strategy.

FLUENCY involves timed reading followed by a comprehension question.

Getting the Total Picture

Your own observation of students' responses and the notes you take, in whatever format, are an essential and invaluable part of assessing each student's progress.

- Observe your students' responses in the daily discussions.
- Circulate in the classroom as they read aloud to each other and as they respond to their independent reading.
- Collect and check two or three Student Guides a day and comment on students' written responses and answers with stick-on notes.

How to Use the Tests

The Informal Reading Inventory

The **Informal Reading Inventory** (IRI), found on page 8, is designed to be administered to each student individually. Each test will take from 1 to 3 minutes, depending on the student's level of reading comprehension and fluency.

The IRI consists of a passage adapted from the AMP Student Guide. The passage is written at a controlled reading level appropriate for students at Level 2. Students will first read the passage silently, then read the passage aloud, and finally, answer three comprehension questions about the passage. During the oral reading, you will evaluate each student's fluency, using the Score Chart for the Informal Reading Inventory found on page 9.

Score Chart for the Informal Reading Inventory

Use the chart (page 9) to record each student's performance. The fluency scores are based on missed words, misread words, and added words. The comprehension score is based on the number of questions the student answered incorrectly.

Administering the Informal Reading Inventory

Make a copy of the Informal Reading Inventory on page 8 for the student. (You might also want to make copies for yourself so you can mark any errors on the passage as you follow students' reading.) Have the student read the passage silently and then aloud. As the student reads aloud, follow carefully and mark any errors either on the Score Chart or on your copy of the page. For each missed word, misread word, or added word, place a tally mark in the appropriate column on the Score Chart or indicate the error on your copy of the passage. Then have the student answer the three comprehension questions by choosing the letter of the correct answer for each question.

After the student completes the IRI, record the results on the Score Chart. Add each tally, and record the number of comprehension items answered incorrectly. Then add the number of missed words, misread words, added words, and comprehension items answered incorrectly and record the total in the appropriate box. Subtract that number from 100 to determine the student's final score. Record the final score in the last column of the chart.

Each student's IRI scores can also be recorded in the **Individual Assessment Record** (page 123).

Assessments

This book contains a Mid-Unit and End-of-Unit Assessment in multiple-choice format for each of the seven units. There are three sections to each Assessment: Vocabulary, Comprehension, and Fluency.

Vocabulary

The Vocabulary section contains 15 questions that test students' understanding of the vocabulary words from the first or second half of a unit.

Comprehension

The Comprehension section contains a 3-page reading passage and 10 comprehension questions that demonstrate (1) students' general comprehension of the passage and (2) their application of the unit comprehension strategy. The passage is written at a controlled Lexile® appropriate for Level 2.

Fluency

The Fluency section contains a one-page reading passage. The number of words in the passage is tracked by the small numbers above the words at intervals of 15 words. Students silently read the passage twice and answer the comprehension question.

Option: For each assessment, or at intervals throughout the year, have each student read the fluency passage aloud as you track any missed words, misread words, or added words.

Administering the Assessments

At the midpoint of a unit (after completing Lesson 9 in the AMP Student Guide and the Pause lesson in the Teacher's Edition), give the **Mid-Unit Assessment** for that unit. At the end of a unit (after completing Lesson 18 and the Reflect lesson), give the **End-of-Unit Assessment** for that unit.

Make a copy of the Assessment for each student. Explain the format to students, and go over each of the three parts with them. Tell them that they will complete **Part 1: Vocabulary** and **Part 2: Comprehension** first. You may want to distribute the Fluency page separately when the class has finished Vocabulary and Comprehension.

For **Part 3: Fluency**, explain to students that they will read the passage once to themselves. They will then wait until you say "start," and read it again. After one minute, say "stop." Students mark the word they were reading at that moment. Then they answer the comprehension question by circling the letter of the correct answer.

Option: Have each student read the passage aloud to you as you follow the procedure used for the Informal Reading Inventory.

Scoring the Assessments

Scoring Guide		
Test section	**Points for each question**	**Total possible score**
Vocabulary	3	45
Comprehension	5	50
Fluency* comprehension	5	5
Total points		100

*The number of words read can be recorded separately on the **Individual Assessment Record**.

To determine the number of words read in the fluency passage by each student, look for the word underlined by the student. Locate the reference number nearest that word. From the reference number count forward to or backward from the underlined word to determine the number of words read.

Recording the Scores

Each student's scores for the Assessments can be recorded in the **Individual Assessment Record** (page 123). Students' scores can also be recorded on the **Class Assessment Record** (page 124).

Informal Reading Inventory

> Cheetahs are the fastest land mammals. They can run at speeds up to 70 miles per hour. Horses are fast, too. They can run up to 50 miles per hour. The horse, like the cheetah, has a powerful heart and lungs. Cheetahs are faster than horses because they have flexible spines. The flexibility in their spines results in a Cheetah's fast whiplike motion. However, a horse would beat a cheetah on a long racetrack because a cheetah tends to stop for breath after about 400 yards. A horse can keep running for miles without stopping for breath. A horse can run for a longer period of time than a cheetah.

Circle the letter of the correct answer to each question.

1. Which of the following explains why a horse can run fast?
   a. It is related to a cheetah.
   b. It has a flexible spine.
   c. Its heart and lungs are powerful.

2. Why is a cheetah faster than a horse?
   a. It has longer legs.
   b. It has a stronger heart.
   c. Its spine is flexible.

3. Why could a horse outrun a cheetah on a long racetrack?
   a. A horse can run for a longer time.
   b. A horse has a stronger heart than a cheetah.
   c. A horse has stronger lungs than a cheetah.

Score Chart for the Informal Reading Inventory

Class _____

Student Name	Missed words		Misread words		Added words		Comprehension items answered incorrectly	Total number of incorrect items	Final score (Subtract incorrect items from 100.)
	Tally	Total #	Tally	Total #	Tally	Total #			

Mid-Unit Assessment
Unit 1

Part 1 Vocabulary

Circle *a* or *b* to answer each question.

1. Can a human *thrive* without food or water?

   a. yes   **b.** no

2. If you have *ample* time before a movie starts, do you need to rush to the theater?

   a. yes   **b.** no

3. Are firefighters considered a *menace* to society?

   a. yes   **b.** no

4. Do fish *inhabit* oceans?

   a. yes   **b.** no

5. When children smile, is it *evident* that they are happy?

   a. yes   **b.** no

Circle the letter of the word that best completes each sentence.

6. Drinking three glasses of water, one after the other, is a _____ amount to drink.

   a. deprived   **b.** substantial   **c.** menace

7. Animals need to _____ to new environments in order to survive.

   a. adapt   **b.** ample   **c.** evident

8. A desert is a specialized _____ made up of certain animals and plants.

   a. endurance   **b.** ecosystem   **c.** nourishment

WORD LIST

adapt

ample

astounding

basically

deprived

ecosystem

endurance

evident

inhabit

menace

migrating

nourishment

relatively

substantial

tend

thrive

Mid-Unit Assessment • Unit 1 continued

9. Craig likes to _____ to injured animals.

    a. menace   **b.** tend   **c.** adapt

10. Running a marathon requires _____.

    a. endurance   **b.** ecosystem   **c.** thrive

11. Doctors do not recommend candy as a form of _____.

    a. migrating   **b.** ample   **c.** nourishment

Circle the letter of the form of the word that correctly completes each sentence.

12. The magician's tricks will _____ you.

    a. astound   **b.** astounding

13. The colors red and scarlet are _____ the same.

    a. relative   **b.** relatively

14. The _____ birds flew from Canada to Mexico.

    a. migrate   **b.** migrating

15. Atoms are studied in chemistry because they are the _____ building blocks for all types of materials.

    a. basically   **b.** basic

Mid-Unit Assessment • Unit 1 continued

Part 2 Comprehension: Summarizing

Read the passage and answer the questions at the end
of the passage.

The Whooping Crane

Whooping cranes are birds that really stand out. Males   1
can grow up to 5 feet tall. This unusual height makes
whooping cranes the tallest birds in North America. Their
bodies are covered with soft, white feathers. The feathers
on their heads are red and black. The tips of their wings
are also black. When they unfold their wings, their wingspan
can be as wide as 7½ feet. These birds got their name
from their unusual calls. They make loud noises that sound
like "whoop!"

Migrating is a part of life for most whooping cranes. It is   2
necessary for their survival. These birds travel south in the
winter when food is hard to find. During migration, adult
birds can fly between 200 and 500 miles per day. They
usually fly at about 47 miles per hour. In the spring, they
fly north again to have offspring.

Meet the Whoopers

Whooping cranes are an endangered species. There   3
are so few of them alive today that they are in danger of
disappearing altogether. In 1860, there were about 1,400
in North America. By 1941, only about 15 were found in
the wild. Hunting and the loss of nesting areas have
caused their population to decline. However, due to
efforts to protect them, their population is now growing.
In 2004, the number of whooping cranes in North America
had grown to 468. Still, whoopers are one of the rarest
birds on this continent.

We Are Families

It is dangerous for whooping cranes in the wild to live in   4
one large flock. The flock could be wiped out by bad weather,
disease, oil spills, or decreasing supplies of fresh water.

Mid-Unit Assessment • Unit 1 continued

To thrive, whoopers must be separated into smaller groups. The smaller groups must live in different locations. This separation increases the whoopers' chances of survival.

The main family of whooping cranes is known as the   5
Western Flock. These whoopers fly south from Canada
to spend the winter months in Texas. Then they fly back
north for the summer to hatch their eggs. These birds are
the only remaining wild flock of whooping cranes that
migrates. In 2004, their population was at 216.

A group of about 100 cranes remains in Florida year-   6
round. They do not migrate. This flock is part of a study
whose goal is to increase the whooping crane population.

A smaller flock of whoopers is the Eastern Flock. These   7
whooping cranes are not wild. They are part of a breeding
program located in Wisconsin. The birds are hatched and
cared for by humans. When the cranes are ready, they are
trained to migrate to Florida. One of the main goals of the
program is to increase the whooping crane population by
helping them migrate safely.

Training to Fly

The migration route for the Eastern Flock is about   8
1,230 miles long. Young whooping cranes living in the wild
follow their parents south in the fall. In the spring, these
young whoopers migrate north on their own. Because the
chicks in the Eastern Flock are raised by humans, they
don't have the ability to migrate on their own. As a result,
they must be taught.

The chicks of the Eastern Flock are trained in a very   9
special way. They learn to follow a small airplane called an
ultralight. As the ultralight flies to a breeding ground in
Florida, the young chicks follow.

How are the chicks trained? Young cranes learn to trust   10
the first object they see, usually their mother. However, the
first thing Eastern Flock chicks see is a human handler
dressed in a whooping crane costume. The chicks learn to
trust the human handler. This unusual method is used to
keep the young birds from becoming attached to humans.
If they did, the birds might think that every human they see
would give them food and care.

Soon after hatching, the chicks are introduced to   11
the ultralight. The costumed handler walks behind the
airplane. The chicks walk behind the handler. After a while,
the chicks become familiar with the ultralight. They will walk
behind the aircraft as it moves slowly. The airplane quickly
becomes the chicks' flight instructor. After many days of
flying lessons to build up their body strength, the birds are
ready to migrate. They fly about 17 miles per day. The trip
takes almost 2 months to complete.

The ultralight is used only for the trip south. During   12
the trip, the young chicks learn the migration route.
Learning the route prepares them to make the return
trip north on their own. In this way, the young cranes
are given freedom and become independent. Eventually,
their ability to migrate safely on their own will help the
whooping crane population grow.

During its first trip in 2001, eight chicks followed an   13
ultralight from Wisconsin to Florida. However, only five
made the return flight to Wisconsin. Since then, many
young cranes have endured this difficult journey and
attempted to live in the wild. Most have been able to
migrate on their own back to Wisconsin for the summer
to lay eggs.

Will There Ever Be Enough?

New cranes are added to the Eastern Flock each fall.   14
They come from other breeding programs. Adding to the
flock is necessary because not all cranes will survive.
There are many reasons why babies might not grow into
adulthood. Some of the young cranes get caught in power
lines along the migration route. Others become sick or are
eaten by predators.

Researchers and scientists hope that the surviving   15
whooping cranes will reproduce and teach their own chicks
to fly. In the meantime, the breeding program continues.
Although costumed handlers and migration with an ultralight
are highly unusual, they are considered the key to increasing
the whooping crane population.

Mid-Unit Assessment • **Unit 1 continued**

1. What is the topic of paragraph 1?

   a. whooping cranes

   b. white birds

   c. tall birds of North America

2. Which of the following is the main idea of paragraph 1?

   a. Whooping cranes have white feathers and are usually tall.

   b. Whooping cranes stand out for several reasons.

   c. Whooping cranes are birds that make unusual noises.

3. How did whooping cranes get their name?

   a. They have unusual calls.

   b. They have a wide wingspan.

   c. They whip their feathers around their body.

4. What is the main idea of the section "We Are Families"?

   a. Many flocks of whooping cranes are raised by humans.

   b. There are different flocks of whooping cranes in North America.

   c. Families of whooping cranes have died due to oil spills.

5. Which is an important detail that supports the main idea of the section "We Are Families?"

   a. *They fly back north for the summer to hatch their eggs.*

   b. *The main family of whooping cranes is known as the Western Flock.*

   c. *In 2004, their population was at 216.*

6. What is the main difference between the Western Flock and the Eastern Flock?

   a. The whooping cranes in the Western Flock are larger and live longer than the cranes in the Eastern Flock.

   b. The Western Flock migrates south in the winter but the Eastern Flock migrates north in the winter.

   c. The Western Flock lives in the wild while the Eastern Flock is raised by humans.

Mid-Unit Assessment • Unit 1 continued

7. What is the main idea of the section "Training to Fly"?

   a. The migration route of the Western Flock is longer than the migration route of the Eastern Flock.

   b. Young Eastern Flock cranes follow an ultralight on their migration to Florida.

   c. Human handlers dress in whooping crane costumes to give the young chicks flying lessons.

8. Why are new cranes added to the Eastern Flock each fall?

   a. because not all cranes will survive

   b. so that they can prepare to follow the ultralight by spring

   c. because some young chicks cannot learn to migrate

9. What is the main idea of the entire passage?

   a. Whooping cranes are highly unusual birds because some migrate but others don't.

   b. Whooping cranes are in danger of disappearing.

   c. There are two families of whooping cranes.

10. Which of the following is the best summary of the entire passage?

   a. The Eastern Flock of whooping cranes are hatched and taught by humans. They follow an ultralight to migrate. Some chicks have returned north on their own.

   b. Whooping cranes are an endangered species. There are different families of whooping cranes. Humans are trying to increase the population of whooping cranes through special breeding and training programs.

   c. The Western Flock of whooping cranes has a better chance of survival in the wild. The Eastern Flock cannot migrate on their own because they have been raised by humans. The Eastern Flock must always depend on humans.

Mid-Unit Assessment • Unit 1 continued

Part 3 Fluency

Read the following passage once. Then read it again as your teacher times you. Underline the word you are reading when your teacher says to stop. Then answer the question.

A salmon begins its life in fresh water. Most salmon breed in fresh
water in the summer or fall. Breeding is also called spawning, and how
salmon spawn is very interesting.

Female salmon lay their eggs in gravel at the bottom of streams or in
the shallow water of lakes. First, a female turns on her side and swishes
her tail around to create a nest in the gravel. The female and male go
into the nest together and swim in place very fast, side-by-side. They look
as though they are dancing. The female releases her eggs, and the male
fertilizes them. Then, the female swims a short distance, creates another
nest, and the male follows. The gravel dug from each nest protects the
eggs that were just laid from predators.

A spawning female lays from 2,000 to 17,000 eggs. It takes from 2 to
7 months for them to hatch. The newborn salmon are called fry. The fry
hide in the gravel nests for several weeks. They get nourishment from the
yolk in their egg sacs. When the yolk is gone, the fry leave their nests to
find food. Some species of salmon stay in fresh water for a long time.
Other kinds of salmon start swimming to the ocean right after they
wriggle out of the gravel.

Which of the following is the topic of the passage?

a. how many eggs female salmon lay

b. how newborn salmon get nourishment

c. how salmon breed

End-of-Unit Assessment
Unit 1

Part 1 Vocabulary

Circle *a* or *b* to answer each question.

1. Is giving a reward an *aspect* of animal training?

    a. yes   **b.** no

2. Does a fever *indicate* how much nourishment a person is getting?

    a. yes   **b.** no

3. If you are *participating* in an event, are you watching from the sidelines?

    a. yes   **b.** no

Circle the letter of the word that best completes each sentence.

4. A wig can _____ a person's appearance.

    a. alter   **b.** interpret   **c.** comprehend

5. The _____ of a plant affects how much sunlight it gets.

    a. factor   **b.** placement   **c.** convey

6. Not everyone will _____ a painting the same way.

    a. indicate   **b.** provoke   **c.** interpret

7. A key part of training pets to do tricks is _____.

    a. exposed   **b.** accurately   **c.** reinforcement

8. Her sister's annoying behavior _____ Sylvia into leaving the room.

    a. altered   **b.** provoked   **c.** demonstrated

WORD LIST

accurately

alter

aspect

comprehend

convey

demonstrate

effective

exposed

factor

indicate

interpret

participating

placement

procedure

provoke

reinforcement

End-of-Unit Assessment • Unit 1 continued

Circle the letter of the word that means almost the same as the word or words in parentheses.

9. (make known) Television is a great way to _____ news because it reaches a large audience.

    a. convey   **b.** provoke   **c.** alter

10. (show) Pet owners often _____ their approval of their pets' behavior by giving them a treat.

    a. effective   **b.** factor   **c.** demonstrate

11. (successful) Brushing and flossing your teeth is an _____ way to prevent cavities.

    a. alter   **b.** effective   **c.** aspect

12. (way of doing something) When an animal follows a _____, it should get rewarded.

    a. factor   **b.** placement   **c.** procedure

Choose the letter of the word that best completes each sentence.

13. *Hidden* is to *evident* as *covered* is to _____.

    a. provoked   **b.** effective   **c.** exposed

14. *Few* is to *many* as *misunderstand* is to _____.

    a. convey   **b.** factor   **c.** comprehend

15. *Alter* is to *change* as *correctly* is to _____.

    a. accurately   **b.** indicate   **c.** demonstrate

Name _____ Date _____

Part 2 Comprehension: Summarizing

Read the passage and answer the questions at the end
of the passage.

Crowd-Pleasing Dolphins

The ball flies through the air. He receives the touchdown   1
pass and flips the ball back to his trainer. He then dives
deep into the water and jumps out with a huge splash! The
audience claps wildly.

Live animal performances can be seen at zoos,   2
aquariums, and theme parks. Dolphins, seals, sea lions,
and whales are among the different kinds of animals that
can be trained to entertain an audience. However, dolphins
are the most popular entertainers. They are also natural
entertainers. Many of the actions they perform for an
audience are the same ones they perform in the open sea.
Dolphins enjoy playful splashing and intelligent chasing
games both in the wild and in front of a cheering crowd.

Dolphins are mammals. There are 35 different species.   3
One of the most familiar is the bottlenose dolphin.
Bottlenose dolphins are gray and are usually between 6 and
9 feet long. The shape of their snouts helped to give them
the name "bottlenose." Bottlenoses are often found in
zoos, aquariums, and theme parks because of their great
ability to adapt. Some bottlenose dolphins are even actors.
They perform in television shows and movies.

Dolphins in Training

Dolphins make excellent students for many reasons.   4
They are strong, intelligent, and curious. They can
understand many sounds and gestures. Research shows
that these animals can even understand simple sentences!

End-of-Unit Assessment • Unit 1 continued

Successful training requires a strong relationship 5
between a dolphin and its trainer. Building a trusting
relationship is very important. The trainer must work
hard to learn about the dolphin's personality. The trainer
watches the dolphin carefully during feedings and playtime
to find out what it enjoys. At the same time, the dolphin
learns what the trainer is like. For example, if a trainer is
very active, the dolphin may adapt and become more playful
and high spirited.

The Method That Works

Most dolphins are trained using positive reinforcement. 6
This method is used when training almost any animal.
When a dolphin does what the trainer wants, it receives a
reward. The dolphin learns to repeat that behavior in order
to get another reward. This type of training is called positive
reinforcement. Usually, the reward is fish. Other rewards
include time with a favorite toy, the sound of the crowd
cheering during a performance, or loving attention from
its trainer.

A target is an object that helps train dolphins to perform 7
a certain behavior. The behavior is taught in small steps.
For example, a ball attached to the end of a pole is often
used as a target. The dolphin is taught to touch the target.
Touching the target earns the dolphin a reward. After the
dolphin learns to touch the target, the target is moved
higher and higher. In this way, the dolphin is taught to jump
higher and higher in order to touch the target. This method
using small steps is called shaping.

Shaping is also used to teach a dolphin how to shake 8
its head no. A trainer gets the dolphin to touch his or her
hand. The trainer then moves his or her hand in a side-to-
side motion. The dolphin's nose follows the direction of the
trainer's hand. In time, the dolphin will learn a signal for
when to shake its head.

During a method called imitation, dolphins are trained 9
to make certain sounds. Because dolphins are sensitive to
sound, they can reproduce certain sounds almost exactly.

End-of-Unit Assessment • Unit 1 continued

Dolphins living in good training facilities are not 10
punished in threatening or harmful ways. Punishment
can ruin the trust needed to effectively train a dolphin.
Instead, dolphins that perform unwanted behaviors are
basically ignored. Ignoring an animal is a form of negative
reinforcement. Trainers just stop what they were doing
and walk away. The dolphin learns not to perform those
behaviors again.

Ready for a Close-Up

Bottlenose dolphins are known for their gentle nature as 11
well as for their intelligence. It is safe for inexperienced
people to spend time in the water with these amazing
animals. Any encounter with dolphins is guaranteed to be
fun and exciting because of their friendly personalities.

Many programs allow people to get close to dolphins. 12
Some programs allow visitors to swim with dolphins. Others
allow the petting and feeding of dolphins. All of these
programs take place under supervised conditions. These
programs are often offered by research centers, aquariums,
and theme parks. Getting close to a dolphin can be an
unforgettable experience.

Circle the letter of the correct answer to each question.

1. What is the main idea of paragraph 1?

   a. A football player receives a pass and scores a
   touchdown.

   b. An audience gets splashed by a clown.

   c. Some kind of water performer entertains a crowd.

2. Why are dolphins natural entertainers?

   a. Because dolphins perform the same actions that
   crowds like in the open sea.

   b. Because dolphins like to play with seals, seal lions,
   and whales in the ocean.

   c. Because they can easily be trained to entertain large crowds.

3. Here is a set of notes about paragraphs 4 and 5:

Title: Crowd-Pleasing Dolphins
Heading and details: Dolphins in Training
1. Dolphins make excellent students because they are strong, intelligent and curious.
2. _____
_____

Which of the following is the missing detail?

a. Research shows that dolphins like to be trained.

b. Dolphins and their trainers must play together a lot.

c. Dolphins and their trainers need to have a strong, trusting relationship.

4. How might a dolphin adapt to a very active trainer?

a. The dolphin might learn faster from the trainer.

b. The dolphin might become more playful.

c. The dolphin might be threatened by the trainer.

5. Which of the following is the topic of the section "The Method That Works."

a. dolphin trainers

b. training dolphins

c. smart dolphins

6. Which is the main idea of the section "The Method That Works"?

a. Dolphins are easy to train because they are not smart.

b. Dolphins are trained using different methods.

c. Some dolphins get rewards and some dolphins get punished.

7. Which is an important detail in "The Method That Works"?

a. *Most dolphins are trained using positive reinforcement.*

b. *The target is moved higher and higher.*

c. *Trainers just stop what they are doing and walk away.*

End-of-Unit Assessment • Unit 1 continued

8. Which is the best summary for the section "The Method
That Works"?

a. Most dolphins are trained using positive reinforcement.
Trainers use a target, shaping, or imitation as methods of
training dolphins.

b. Dolphins that do not respond to training are not
punished. Punishing a dolphin can ruin the
relationship between a dolphin and its trainer.

c. Dolphins are very smart animals that can be trained
to jump high into the air and imitate certain sounds.
Dolphins should be rewarded only with fish.

9. Which is an example of positive reinforcement?

a. imitation

b. time with a favorite toy

c. the trainer's hand

10. Which of the following is the best summary for the
entire passage?

a. Dolphins, seals, sea lions, and whales can all be
trained to entertain audiences. These animals are
easily trained because they are intelligent. They also
perform the same actions in the open sea.

b. Dolphins are intelligent animals that can be trained.
Trainers use a variety of methods, but most include both
positive and negative reinforcement. Because dolphins
are gentle animals, some programs allow physical contact
with them.

c. To train any animal, a trainer should use positive reinforcement.
A trainer should never punish an animal. Instead, he or she
should use negative reinforcement. A trainer must establish a
trusting relationship with the animal he or she is training.

End-of-Unit Assessment • Unit 1 continued

Part 3 Fluency

Read the following passage once. Then read it again as your teacher times you. Underline the word you are reading when your teacher says to stop. Then answer the question.

A camel is a calm animal, but it can be stubborn. Camels often
grumble when they are provoked or when they are made to work.

Training a camel is something like training a horse. However,
Dr. Charmian Wright, who trains camels, says that there is something
camels respond to better than horses do: food!

Dr. Wright is a veterinarian in Utah, as well as an expert camel
trainer. You may be wondering why a camel trainer can be found in the
United States, when most camels used for work are found in Africa and
the Middle East. Actually, there are some camels living in the United
States, too. Dr. Wright takes groups of people on camel rides in the Utah
desert. She has trained all of her camels herself. They are so well trained,
they have even been in movies!

Because camels are so stubborn, Dr. Wright starts out slowly when
she trains them. She uses the following procedure. First, she holds out a
pan of grain and lets the camel eat. Meanwhile, she pets the camel's neck
and head to convey that the camel can trust her. Just getting the camel to
let her touch it while it is eating may take Dr. Wright weeks of daily or
twice-daily lessons.

Which of the following is the main idea of the passage?
a. Camels are stubborn but can be trained.
b. Dr. Wright starts slowly when training camels.
c. Camels can be found in the United States.

Mid-Unit Assessment
Unit 2

Part 1 Vocabulary
Circle *a* or *b* to answer each question.

WORD LIST

assortment
courtesy
define
dispose
distracted
eligible
omit
preoccupied
recede
reject
resident
sluggish
spontaneously
summon
survey
valid

1. Is it a good idea to *dispose* of trash?

    a. yes   **b.** no

2. To write a good report, should you *omit* important details?

    a. yes   **b.** no

3. Do you pay close attention when you are *distracted*?

    a. yes   **b.** no

4. If you don't get enough rest, might you feel *sluggish*?

    a. yes   **b.** no

Circle the letter of the word that means almost the same as the underlined word or words.

5. Only trained athletes are <u>qualified</u> to compete.

    a. distracted   **b.** eligible   **c.** preoccupied

6. When the clown <u>suddenly</u> stepped in a bucket of water, the children burst into laughter.

    a. courtesy   **b.** sluggish   **c.** spontaneously

7. The committee will <u>refuse</u> applications that are handed in late.

    a. recede   **b.** reject   **c.** summon

8. Please <u>say exactly</u> the purpose of your paper.

    a. define   **b.** survey   **c.** summon

9. When the tide <u>pulls back</u>, it leaves many shells exposed on the shore.

    a. recedes   **b.** omits   **c.** defines

Mid-Unit Assessment • Unit 2 continued

Circle the letter of the form of the word that correctly completes each sentence.

10. The principal thanked the students for their _____ during the assembly.

    a. discourtesy **b.** courtesy

11. Tim needs a _____ password in order to use the computer.

    a. valid   **b.** invalid

12. Elaine didn't join in the fun because she was _____ with her project.

    a. unoccupied **b.** preoccupied

13. The _____ put the items into different boxes.

    a. sorter   **b.** assorted   **c.** assortment

14. The place where you live is your _____.

    a. reside   **b.** resident   **c.** residence

15. The police department has the suspect under _____.

    a. survey   **b.** surveyor   **c.** surveillance

Mid-Unit Assessment • Unit 2 continued

Part 2 Comprehension: Questioning

Read the passage and answer the questions at the end
of the passage.

All Nations to the Rescue

It was late December 2004. Many people were working
or relaxing on beaches throughout Southeast Asia. They
were unaware of the activity far out at sea. This activity was
taking place under the ocean floor. Suddenly, the ocean
floor buckled in an underwater earthquake!   1

The quake rocked the waters of the Indian Ocean. It
gave rise to a menacing wall of water called a tsunami.
The height of the tsunami was more than 30 feet. Before
people could be warned, the deadly wall of seawater
crashed onto the shores of Indonesia, Thailand, Sri Lanka,
and other areas in Asia. It even flooded the shores of some
countries in East Africa.   2

What was left when the water receded? Where seaside
villages once stood, only mud and debris remained. More
than 200,000 people were killed. Many thousands were
missing. More than 1 million people were left homeless. It
was the most destructive tsunami in recorded history.   3

The World Responds

Soon after the tsunami hit, help began to arrive from
around the world. The United Nations (UN) immediately
sent emergency funds and food to the places in need.
Governments of countries everywhere gave billions of
dollars in aid. Even a small African country—one of the
world's poorest countries—donated $100,000! People and
private companies from around the world sent donations to
relief organizations. These relief organizations included the
Red Cross and UNICEF. An astounding amount of money
was collected for the tsunami victims. However, money is
not all that people gave.   4

Within days, volunteers began to arrive. People at the disaster scene witnessed a worldwide rescue effort. What did that effort look like? Airplanes from Australia, Spain, and other countries landed with food and medical supplies. An American hospital ship pulled into port to treat injured people. Rescue helicopters from Russia, Mexico, and South Africa flew over the area in search of survivors. Heavy equipment from Singapore began clearing debris from roads. Much work was getting done, but help was coming too fast. There was a lot of confusion. It was evident that the relief workers needed a plan.

5

World leaders met and decided that the UN should direct operations. From then on, the rescue became more organized. Planners made sure food and medical supplies reached people in all parts of the disaster area. Organizers gave top priority to providing clean water. Air traffic controllers from the Netherlands arrived to keep order in the skies as hundreds of flights arrived with supplies.

6

Rebuilding Everyday Life

Thousands of tsunami victims lost everything they owned. Drinking water was contaminated. Food was soaked and spoiled. People could not get things they needed to start over because stores, farms, and fishing boats had been washed away. To help people rebuild their lives, volunteers from the Red Cross and other relief groups brought in tons of supplies. They distributed food and set up tanks of clean drinking water. Also among the supplies given were tents for shelter and kits for daily living. The kits contained bedding, mosquito netting, pots, pans, plates, lanterns, soap, shampoo, and toothbrushes.

7

To help children, volunteers set up large tents in which orphans could be cared for. They also organized temporary schools. Each student received an assortment of school supplies. These supplies included a notebook, pencils, erasers, a sharpener, paints, and crayons. After losing everything, the little bags of school supplies made the children feel better. The familiar routine of school also helped them feel less anxious and afraid.

8

Mid-Unit Assessment • Unit 2 continued

Children were not the only ones who felt afraid. Many 9
people had trouble sleeping or feeling safe. They kept
remembering the terrible tsunami and the destruction it
caused. Some people were preoccupied with the idea that
another tsunami would hit. Volunteer counselors from many
countries stepped in and helped victims deal with their fears.

Building a Future

Though a lot of help and ample supplies were available, 10
the rebuilding of these disaster areas would take time.
Debris was everywhere. Thousands of buildings and roads
needed to be rebuilt. People were living in temporary
shelters in crowded camps. They needed homes and jobs.
The victims of the tsunami were surviving, but how would
they ever build a life with a hopeful future?

As weeks went by, the UN, Red Cross, and other relief 11
groups started new programs to get victims back on their
feet. Fishermen received grants to buy fishing gear and to
rebuild their boats. Thousands of local people were hired to
help dispose of the debris. Some people were given
construction jobs building better shelters at the camps.
Many workers were allowed to keep the tools they used on
the job. These programs provided residents of Southeast
Asia with money and tools to rebuild their homes,
businesses, and communities.

The people of Southeast Asia suffered terrible losses as 12
a result of the tsunami. It will take years of work to repair
their lives and communities. However, the victims know
they will not work alone. As they build their future, their
neighbors around the world will be there to help.

Mid-Unit Assessment • Unit 2 continued

Circle the letter of the correct answer to each question.

1. Which is a good goal-setting question for this passage?

   a. Will another tsunami strike the coast of Southeast Asia?

   b. How did the nations of the world come to the rescue?

   c. How many buildings were destroyed by the tsunami?

2. Why didn't people leave the area before the tsunami hit?

   a. They did not hear the warning.

   b. There was no warning.

   c. They believed that the earthquake was too far out at sea to affect them.

3. Which question is answered in paragraph 2?

   a. How far away is East Africa from Southeast Asia?

   b. How deep is the Indian Ocean?

   c. Which areas were affected by the tsunami?

4. Which of the following is a "between the lines" question for paragraph 4?

   a. Where is the very poor country that donated to the rescue effort located?

   b. Why would one of the world's poorest countries give money to tsunami victims?

   c. How much money was donated to the tsunami victims by one of the poorest countries in the world?

5. Which question is answered in paragraph 6?

   a. How did the United Nations end the confusion involved in relief efforts?

   b. How much money did foreign countries donate to the relief effort?

   c. How much food and drinking water was supplied to the victims of the tsunami?

Mid-Unit Assessment • Unit 2 continued

6. Why did relief supplies have to be shipped in from other places?

    a. Stores and services had been wiped out by the tsunami.

    b. Victims had no money to buy the items locally.

    c. Local supplies were being reserved in case of another tsunami.

7. Which of the following is a good goal-setting question for the section "Rebuilding Everyday Life"?

    a. How will tsunami victims live normal lives again?

    b. Who lives in the large tents?

    c. How are houses built in the areas affected by the tsunami?

8. Which question can you answer by reading "between the lines" of paragraph 8?

    a. What subjects did volunteers teach in the temporary schools they set up?

    b. Why did going to school make children feel better after the tsunami?

    c. How did volunteers decide what school supplies to provide for students?

9. Which is NOT a way that the UN and the Red Cross helped tsunami victims get back on their feet?

    a. giving grants for rebuilding boats

    b. giving jobs cleaning up debris

    c. giving cash for used tools

10. How will the communities of Southeast Asia be repaired?

    a. The UN will rebuild all the homes, schools, and communities.

    b. People throughout the world will help.

    c. The UN will provide all the money and supplies that will be needed.

Mid-Unit Assessment • Unit 2 continued

Part 3 Fluency

Read the following passage once. Then read it again as your teacher times you. Underline the word you are reading when your teacher says to stop. Then answer the question.

Search dogs and their owners, or handlers, are trained to rescue people.

While search dogs are in training, their handlers also take an intensive 6-day

training course. Handlers are usually firefighters or other first responders.

The staff members of the National Disaster Search Dog Foundation

carefully match dogs and their handlers. Staff members consider the

personalities and learning styles of each dog and handler. After a match is

made, each new team spends 10 more days at the training kennel together.

They practice the skills they've learned so they can work together in the future.

Finally, the dog and handler go home together to begin their new life as

a disaster search team. The team practices what they've learned on a daily

basis. They are careful not to omit any skills. They also have frequent

training "tune-ups" to make sure they don't forget any of their newly

acquired skills.

Dogs must pass a test before they can become valid search dogs for

urban, or city, search and rescue operations. This 3-hour test "certifies" the

dog. During the test, a dog has 20 minutes to find 6 volunteers who pose as

victims buried in three massive piles of rubble. The dog must avoid

distractions. For example, a dog must reject all scents other than the scent

of a live victim. The test is also a challenge for the handler. He or she must

read the dog's cues in order to pinpoint the location of the victims.

Which of the following questions is answered in the selection?

a. What kinds of dogs do not make good search dogs?

b. What are some skills that search dogs need to become "certified"?

c. What kind of test do handlers have to pass to become "certified"?

End-of-Unit Assessment
Unit 2

Part 1 Vocabulary

Circle *a* or *b* to answer each question.

WORD LIST
accumulate
adjacent
advocate
appreciation
ascend
brink
climax
contrivance
devote
display
extract
grimy
reduce
resistance
tragic
weaken

1. Is the *climax* of a story usually the most exciting part?

    a. yes   **b.** no

2. Should a hospital floor be *grimy*?

    a. yes   **b.** no

3. Is a five-year-old child's birthday party a *tragic* event?

    a. yes   **b.** no

4. When an airplane takes off, does it *ascend* into the sky?

    a. yes   **b.** no

5. Does the person *adjacent* to you in class sit next to you?

    a. yes   **b.** no

Circle the letter of the word that best completes each sentence.

6. The cat showed _____ to her food by knocking over her feeding bowl.

    a. resistance   **b.** display   **c.** contrivance

7. Joanne put ice on her sprained ankle to _____ the swelling.

    a. weaken   **b.** extract   **c.** reduce

8. A lot of dust will _____ on the trunk if you put it in the attic.

    a. ascend   **b.** devote   **c.** accumulate

End-of-Unit Assessment • Unit 2 continued

9. Les showed his _____ to his grandmother by sending her flowers.

    a. extract   **b.** resistance   **c.** appreciation

10. The mayor _____ a ban on smoking in restaurants.

    a. advocates   **b.** devotes   **c.** weakens

11. My dentist said that she needed to _____ the broken tooth.

    a. reduce   **b.** ascend   **c.** extract

Circle the letter of the word that has the same meaning as the underlined word or words.

12. The car stopped before the <u>edge</u> of the cliff.

    a. brink   **b.** climax   **c.** appreciation

13. The lack of exercise can cause your body to <u>lose strength</u>.

    a. reduce   **b.** weaken   **c.** advocate

14. Mario decided to <u>give</u> his time to helping stray animals.

    a. display   **b.** ascend   **c.** devote

15. Please <u>show</u> your art projects in the school gym.

    a. weaken   **b.** display   **c.** contrivance

End-of-Unit Assessment • Unit 2 continued

Part 2 Comprehension: Questioning

Read the passage and answer the questions at the end of the passage.

Coal Mining in America

What do you picture when you think of a workplace? It's   1
easy to imagine an indoor job in a store or office. It's not
hard to picture an outdoor job in a construction business.
What would it be like to work underground?

A coal mine is a workplace unlike any other. It is dark   2
and wet. It has a strong smell of coal. The damp surfaces
are slippery, and the air may contain poisonous gases. At
any moment, the roof could fall in. A mine is filled with
many dangers. Still, millions of Americans have made their
living in this underground workplace.

Early Days of Mining

Coal is a source of fuel. Today, the greatest use of coal   3
is to produce electricity. Coal can be found underground in
large areas called coal beds. In many areas of the United
States, extensive mining for coal took place in the 1850s.
During that time, coal was used as fuel for steam engines
and furnaces. Coal mines could be found in West Virginia,
Pennsylvania, Tennessee, Utah, and Illinois.

The workday was harsh for early American miners. They   4
worked a 10-hour day starting at sunup. Adult men were
paid about $1.50 a day. Boys as young as 12 years old
worked the same long hours for only $.50 a day. The work
was grimy and exhausting.

The youngest workers started out as breaker boys. They   5
worked in buildings called coal breakers. In coal breakers,
large lumps of coal were broken apart and sorted. The
breaker boys sat on hard benches and cleaned the coal as
it tumbled down a narrow ramp. All day long, they leaned
over the ramp and picked out the sharp lumps of coal.
Their hands became bruised and raw.

End-of-Unit Assessment • Unit 2 continued

When they were older, the boys worked the mine doors. 6
They opened and closed the heavy mine doors to let miners
and coal cars pass through. It was a lonely, boring job. The
boys hoped to become drivers. A driver's job was to hitch
the mules to empty coal cars each morning and lead them
into the mine. When the cars were full, the drivers led the
mules back out of the mine.

The oldest, most experienced boys were eligible to 7
become laborers. They loaded the cars with coal that the
miners blasted and chipped loose from the mine.

All the boys lived for the day they would become real 8
miners. When they got the job, they had to buy a lamp and
all their tools. They also supplied their own dynamite. Except
for the work the dynamite did, all the miner's work was done
by hand. A miner made holes in the mine walls with a hand
drill for the placement of the dynamite. He also used a pick
ax, hammer, and crowbar to break up lumps of coal.

Being a miner was a big responsibility and a dangerous 9
job. A miner had to help prop up the roof of the mine with
wooden beams. Then, he would help decide which areas
were the best places to blast. However, one wrong decision
could cause a deadly cave-in. There were also dangers
the miners couldn't control. If they got near a pocket of
methane gas, the flame of their lamps could cause an
explosion. Underground water could weaken the mine and
cause a collapse. Perhaps the most dangerous part of the
job was that every day, miners breathed in coal dust that
often lead to disease and death.

After a cave-in or explosion, a rescue was difficult. It 10
was hard, slow work clearing blocked tunnels with hand
tools. Rescuers often didn't know which tunnel to clear.
There was no way to communicate with trapped miners.
Sadly, more than a thousand miners died in accidents
each year.

Modern Mining

Today, a miner's job is very different. Work conditions 11
are safer and healthier than ever before. Much of the work
is done with high-tech equipment and computers. Many
modern miners are engineers that have college degrees.
Some of these miners are the highest-paid industrial
workers in the United States.

End-of-Unit Assessment • Unit 2 continued

What makes today's mines safer than earlier ones? For one thing, computers, global positioning satellites, and lasers are used in choosing locations for tunnels. These high-tech inventions help engineers avoid areas where the ground is weak. Underground water can also be avoided. The same technology helps locate trapped miners if there ever is an accident. **12**

Being inside a mine is safer, too. Steel structures are bolted to the roof of a mine. The walls of the mine are covered in powdered white rock. The powder settles the coal dust so miners breathe in less of it. Huge fans move fresh air into the mine and blow out dangerous gases. **13**

Miners also wear a lot of personal safety equipment. Hard hats, steel-toed boots, hearing protection, and high-intensity lights are standard equipment. Miners carry monitors that detect methane gas. They also carry a filter to breathe through if they encounter the toxic gas. **14**

Modern equipment makes mining safer and easier. Gone are the days of the pick ax and shovel! Instead, a machine called a continuous miner breaks coal loose from mine walls. It also loads coal onto a moving belt. The belt transports the coal to another area of the mine. Drills and dynamite are no longer needed. **15**

There are also mine safety programs. An important part of these programs is maintaining mine rescue stations. These emergency service stations are equipped with the tools and devices needed to rescue trapped miners. Trained professional rescue teams are on call at these stations 24 hours a day. **16**

Although a mine is still a dangerous place, the risk of injury on the job is now much lower than it has ever been. Safer standards and modern technology have made this underground workplace a safer environment. In fact, the risk of injury for a mine worker is now about the same as the risk of injury for a grocery store worker. **17**

End-of-Unit Assessment • Unit 2 continued

Circle the letter of the correct answer to each question.

1. Which is the best goal-setting question for this passage?
   a. What is it like to work inside a coal mine?
   b. Why didn't girls work in coal mines?
   c. How many coal mines are there in the United States?

2. Why is a coal mine a dangerous workplace?
   a. It is located underground.
   b. There is risk of injury.
   c. Dynamite is stored there.

3. Which is a good "beyond the text" question for paragraph 2?
   a. How would it feel to be inside a coal mine?
   b. Why would the roof of a mine fall in?
   c. What are some jobs that miners do?

4. Which job did young boys working in coal mines have?
   a. They helped to make holes in the mine walls for placement of dynamite.
   b. They used a pick ax, hammer, and crowbar to break up coal.
   c. They picked coal from a narrow ramp and cleaned the coal.

5. Why did the author describe the work that young boys did in a coal mine?
   a. to show that long ago, boys did not go to school
   b. to show that young boys worked hard at an early age
   c. to show that girls did not work in coal mines

End-of-Unit Assessment • Unit 2 continued

6. Which was NOT a responsibility of an early miner?

a. using computers to locate trapped miners

b. helping to prop up the roof of the mine

c. making holes in mine walls using hand drills

7. Which is a good goal-setting question for the section "Modern Mining"?

a. Where are coal mines located today?

b. At what age are boys eligible to become miners?

c. How are mines today different from how they used to be?

8. Which is a "between the lines" question for paragraph 13?

a. Why are the walls of a mine covered with powdered white rock?

b. What does a steel structure bolted to the roof of a coal mine do?

c. What is the purpose of using a huge fan inside a coal mine?

9. Which is one way modern mining is different from the early days of mining?

a. Modern mining doesn't require men to go into coal mines.

b. Modern mining uses technology to rescue trapped miners.

c. Modern mines don't have toxic gases inside them.

10. Why did the author compare mining to working in a grocery store?

a. to emphasize that mining is not as pleasant as working indoors

b. to help readers understand how safe mining is today

c. to help readers visualize how large and modern mines are

End-of-Unit Assessment • Unit 2 continued

Part 3 Fluency

Read the following passage once. Then read it again as your teacher times you. Underline the word you are reading when your teacher says to stop. Then answer the question.

Excitement built as the drill neared a depth of 240 feet. Mining officials
knew that was where the drill would break through the mine roof. Everyone
prepared for the dramatic climax. Ambulances and emergency equipment sat
ready at the site. News reporters and photographers were also on hand. People
tried to stay hopeful, although no one knew for sure if the miners were still
alive. One rescue worker said, "We are approaching the moment of truth."

That moment finally arrived on Saturday night at 10:15 p.m. Seven of
the trapped men were resting on the mine floor, trying to stay warm. Two of
the trapped men, walking in the mine passageway, saw the opening made
by the drill. "We found the hole!" One of the men shouted.

Miners raced to the rescue hole and yelled upward, "Get us out! Help
us! Please get us out!"

Rescue workers couldn't hear the shouting from so far away. However,
they did hear the tapping when the miners banged on the drill. The excited
workers did not display their emotions. The rescuers resisted showing their
excitement because they did not want to draw the attention of news
reporters. The governor had ordered that the miners' families learn of any
new developments before reporters broadcast them. Quietly, word spread
among mining officials that noise was coming from the mine.

Which question is answered by important details in the passage?

a. Where was the mine that the men were trapped in located?

b. How did the miners' families react after the rescue?

c. Why didn't the rescue workers show any emotion when they heard tapping?

Mid-Unit Assessment
Unit 3

Part 1 Vocabulary
Circle *a* or *b* to answer each question.

WORD LIST

apparatus

compact

comparatively

crucial

data

enclosure

exceptional

generate

investigate

isolated

monitor

nonetheless

penetrate

probe

speculate

transmit

1. Are you *isolated* on a crowded bus?

   a. yes   **b.** no

2. Can you use the Internet to collect *data*?

   a. yes   **b.** no

3. Is a microscope an *apparatus* you would find in a science lab?

   a. yes   **b.** no

4. Is candy a *crucial* part of a healthy diet?

   a. yes   **b.** no

Circle the letter of the word that best completes each sentence.

5. Doctors _____ their patients' condition using special equipment.

   a. speculate   **b.** monitor   **c.** comparatively

6. We traded in our _____ car for a van that we all fit into.

   a. compact   **b.** crucial   **c.** nonetheless

7. Our group hopes to _____ lots of ideas during our meeting.

   a. speculate   **b.** monitor   **c.** generate

8. Michael's singing is _____ partly because he practices every single day.

   a. exceptional   **b.** isolated   **c.** crucial

Mid-Unit Assessment • Unit 3 continued

9. The space _____ orbited Saturn to gather information and take pictures.

    a. data   **b.** compact   **c.** probe

10. The radio and receiver were down all day so nobody could receive or _____ messages.

    a. data   **b.** penetrate   **c.** transmit

11. Put the dog back in the _____ so he doesn't run away again.

    a. nonetheless   **b.** enclosure   **c.** data

12. Our puppy was _____ smaller than the other dogs in the litter.

    a. compact   **b.** isolated   **c.** comparatively

Circle the letter of the form of the word that correctly completes each sentence.

13. The _____ of the nail through the wood caused the wood to split.

    a. penetrate   **b.** penetration

14. I didn't know why Maria was absent so I could only _____.

    a. speculate   **b.** speculation

15. The detective wanted to _____ the crime scene to look for clues.

    a. investigate   **b.** investigation

Mid-Unit Assessment • Unit 3 continued

Part 2 Comprehension: Predicting

Read the passage and answer the questions at the end
of the passage.

Going for a Spin

The spacecraft shook as it tilted up and down. The 1
anxious crew gripped the arms of their chairs as the
captain furiously tried to gain control of the ship. "Mission
control, can you read me?" Jackie shouted into the
intercom. "We are having a computer malfunction." She
heard static and crackling in her headset and then she
heard nothing at all. It was no use—all contact with Earth
was gone.

"We are approaching the black hole," Jackie shouted to 2
the crew. "We can try to contact Mission Control again or
we can let the ship veer off course. If we veer, we may be
able to avoid the pull of the black hole. But that means the
computer system will go dead. I think it's our only chance
though to keep from being sucked into the black hole."

"It's too risky!" said the copilot. "We might avoid the 3
black hole, but we'll still be in trouble. Without a working
computer to monitor us and keep us on course, our
chances of reaching Earth are about one in 300 billion."
The copilot continued, "We need Mission Control to guide
us away from the black hole. They can tell us how to fix the
computer malfunctions. Let's keep trying to contact them."
The crew turned toward Jackie and waited for her decision.
"It's your call, Captain, but we have to act quickly. What do
you want us to do?" Jackie froze in panic.

Just then, a bright light filled the room. "Wake up, 4
ladies," said Ms. Harper, one of the space academy
instructors. "Get suited up and ready for breakfast." Jackie
blinked and rubbed the sleep from her eyes as she glanced
at the clock on the wall. In 20 minutes, she and the other
students would be starting day three of space training.

After breakfast, everyone crowded into a simulation   5
room. Jackie stared with uneasiness at a spinning chair
suspended in the air. The chair was surrounded by several
large rings and tumbled this way and that. It even turned
upside down. "What you see here," said an instructor, "is
our Multi-Axis Trainer. This chair will test your ability to cope
with the pitching and rolling of a space ship in distress, and
is a crucial part of astronaut training. Each of you will climb
aboard, get strapped in, and spend 3 minutes in this chair."

Jackie gulped and moved to the back of the line. Just   6
watching the chair spin made her sick to her stomach. At
that moment, Jackie's twin brother Peter volunteered to be
first. He climbed aboard the apparatus with excitement and
ease. His confidence and enthusiasm made Jackie feel
even worse. An instructor fastened safety straps around
Peter's ankles, legs, and shoulders. Peter gave a thumbs up
to his sister as the chair began to spin.

Jackie watched Peter tilt and spin in every direction.   7
He actually seemed to enjoy the dizzying motion. Jackie
thought about how different they were. Peter was the active
type who could barely sit still in school. On the other hand,
Jackie always did an exceptional job in school and earned
the highest marks in the seventh grade. However, space
training was not exactly like school. In fact, the first two
days had zapped Jackie's confidence. Jackie excelled at the
classroom subjects, but every simulation or field-training
task was a near disaster.

Her bad luck started the first day at the space academy.   8
Jackie, Peter, and their team worked together to design
their robot. Jackie did the calculations and entered the data
into the computer. One by one, each team performed its
task. Each robot moved across the room, picked up an egg,
and gently placed it in a basket without breaking the egg.
When it was her team's turn, Jackie started the computer
program and their robot moved across the floor and picked
up an egg. Then it picked up another egg and another. In
fact, it picked up every egg and tried to put each one into
the basket. The next thing Jackie knew, there were cracked
eggs all over the floor!

Mid-Unit Assessment • Unit 3 continued

The second day was no better. Everyone put on space 9
suits and performed simple exercises in a low-gravity
environment. However, Jackie tripped on the balance beam
and fell while running through an obstacle course. She even
had trouble opening her pouch of space food. On her fifth
attempt, she finally ripped it open, but the contents sprayed
all over the front of her helmet.

Jackie felt a tap on her shoulder. "Ready to take a 10
spin?" asked Peter. "I know what you're thinking," he said.
"But it really looks worse than it feels."

"Easy for you to say," replied Jackie. "Just about 11
everything I've done has gone wrong." She watched as the
next person climbed into the Multi-Axis Trainer. "I don't
know about this. What if I throw up?"

"Then you clean yourself up." said Peter. "Besides, you 12
can't quit now. You're the team captain."

Jackie looked at Peter in disbelief. How could he have 13
possibly known about her nightmare about being captain?
"How did you know?" she asked her brother.

"Know about what?" Peter asked. "Anyway, I nominated 14
you for space shuttle captain and the rest of the team
agrees." Jackie couldn't believe her ears. "Without you,"
Peter continued, "we would never get anything done. You're
the organizer."

"But most of our tasks have gone wrong," said Jackie. 15

"Yeah, I know." Peter said. "But you always know how to 16
fix them afterward. Remember our robot and the eggs all
over the floor?"

Jackie hadn't really thought about it that way, but Peter 17
was right. After a few adjustments to the computer, Jackie
had the robot working perfectly. She grinned, "I guess I am
good at figuring things out," she then said, "I suppose it's
time for me to take a spin." Peter watched Jackie as she
walked toward the Multi-Axis Trainer.

Mid-Unit Assessment • Unit 3 continued

Circle the letter of the correct answer to each question.

1. Which kind of event was occurring in paragraphs 1, 2, and 3?

   a. a launch of a spacecraft

   b. a simulation at a space academy

   c. a nightmare

2. Which of the following is a good prediction based on Jackie's reaction to the Multi-Axis Trainer?

   a. Jackie won't get on it.

   b. Jackie will be the first to volunteer to sit in it.

   c. Jackie will fix it.

3. What do you predict the instructor wants the students to learn from the Multi-Axis Trainer?

   a. how it feels inside a space ship in distress

   b. how it feels to command a mission and a crew

   c. how it feels to be dizzy and sick

4. Which of the following would probably have happened if Peter's safety straps hadn't worked?

   a. The instructor would have been angry at him.

   b. He would have broken the chair.

   c. He would have gotten hurt.

5. When Peter says "I know what you're thinking," what does he predict that Jackie is thinking?

   a. that she is jealous of him

   b. that she doesn't want to get into the chair

   c. that she can't wait for it to be her turn

Mid-Unit Assessment • Unit 3 continued

6. Why did Jackie stare at Peter in disbelief?

   a. Because he told her that she was the space shuttle captain.

   b. Because the robot broke the eggs.

   c. Because he was the first to volunteer to sit in the Multi-Axis Trainer.

7. Why did Jackie lack confidence at camp?

   a. Because Peter attended camp with her.

   b. Because many things were going wrong.

   c. Because her group members didn't like her.

8. Based on paragraph 9, what can the reader conclude about Jackie?

   a. Jackie is athletic.

   b. Jackie is curious.

   c. Jackie is clumsy.

9. Which of the following is a good prediction about what Jackie will do after she walks to the Multi-Axis Trainer?

   a. climb aboard and ride in the chair

   b. ask the instructor if she can be excused

   c. nominate Peter for captain

10. Which of the following would be the best choice for another title for this story?

   a. The Trouble With Twins

   b. A Real Leader

   c. How to Fix a Robot

Mid-Unit Assessment • Unit 3 continued

Part 3 Fluency

Read the following passage once. Then read it again as your teacher times you. Underline the word you are reading when your teacher says to stop. Then answer the question.

In 1961, President Kennedy told the United States that it was time to
prepare for "landing a man on the Moon and returning him safely to Earth."
He said this would take less than 10 years. A rocket had to be built that
could carry astronauts the 250,000 miles to the Moon. Ten years was a tight
deadline for such a complex mission. Scientists got right to work. They
called the job the Apollo mission.

First, scientists had to understand the conditions on the Moon. This
information was crucial in helping astronauts to be safe when they landed
there. Many spacecraft were launched. The first set of spacecraft flew
around the Moon. The information sent back helped scientists to generate
maps of the Moon. Soon they were able to select possible landing sites.

Next, another set of spacecraft landed on the Moon and tested its
surface. The data sent back showed that a spacecraft could land on the
Moon's surface and not sink. Finally scientists also had to figure out how to
send people so far into space. They began building a super-powerful rocket.
The rocket could lift and boost a spacecraft to the Moon. People had to live
in the spacecraft for up to 2 weeks. This is how long the trip takes.

What can you predict happened after scientists built the
super-powerful rocket?

a. They tested whether humans could live in a spacecraft for two weeks.

b. President Kennedy canceled the Apollo mission because it
was too dangerous.

c. Lots of people made plans to travel to the Moon for two weeks.

End-of-Unit Assessment
Unit 3

Part 1 Vocabulary

Circle *a* or *b* to answer each question.

1. Is there *merit* in not taking care of a pet?

   a. yes   **b.** no

2. Is doing your best in school a good *objective*?

   a. yes   **b.** no

3. Should you *ration* your money so that you don't spend it all at once?

   a. yes   **b.** no

4. Does the temperature stay *unchanged* every day?

   a. yes   **b.** no

Circle the letter of the word that best completes each sentence.

5. Sasha will _____ me with the science experiment.

   a. assist   **b.** announce   **c.** evaluate

6. I feel _____ to be the best soccer player I can possibly be.

   a. unchanged   **b.** compelled   **c.** exceeding

7. _____ is difficult if the map that you are using is wrong.

   a. Navigation   **b.** Merit   **c.** Evaluate

8. The stormy conditions are _____ for a picnic.

   a. objective   **b.** compelled   **c.** unfavorable

WORD LIST

- acceptable
- announce
- assist
- assumption
- compelled
- evaluate
- exceeding
- merit
- navigation
- objective
- presumably
- ration
- specialized
- technically
- unchanged
- unfavorable

End-of-Unit Assessment • Unit 3 continued

9. The team's excellent performance this year is _____ everyone's predictions.

    a. assist   **b.** merit   **c.** exceeding

10. Maria will _____ the computer to decide if it will be a good purchase.

    a. unchanged   **b.** ration   **c.** evaluate

Circle the letter of the form of the word that correctly completes each sentence.

11. I wrote my homework neatly so my teacher would say it looked _____.

    a. accept   **b.** acceptable   **c.** acceptance

12. My brother wants to _____ his good news at the dinner table.

    a. announce   **b.** announcer   **c.** announcement

13. I _____ that Diego is angry by the tone of his voice.

    a. assume   **b.** assumable   **c.** assumption

14. The wheelchair's extra features were designed by a _____.

    a. specialized   **b.** specialist   **c.** special

15. Our new television is more _____ advanced than our old one.

    a. technical   **b.** technically **c.** technician

End-of-Unit Assessment • Unit 3 continued

Part 2 Comprehension: Predicting

Read the passage and answer the questions at the end of the passage.

Twin Travelers

Two travelers soar through space at an incredible speed. [1] They dodge asteroids and ice. Scientists on Earth watch through cameras attached to the travelers. Will they make it to their target safely? What will they find? The travelers race through the vast darkness of space. They approach swirling clouds that surround a huge gas giant. This giant is the planet Saturn. It is circled by beautiful rings. Yet these rings are not solid. They are made up of pieces of ice, dust, and rock. An orange moon looms in the distance. It is Titan, Saturn's largest moon. Finally, the two travelers reach their target.

What are the names of these space travelers? They [2] are Cassini and Huygens. These travelers are not human. Cassini and Huygens are two space probes. In 1997, the identical probes were launched into space together. The launch was no easy task because together they weigh about 6 tons. Three space agencies, one in the United States, another in France, and a third in Italy, were determined to succeed. They wanted to find out more about Saturn and its moon Titan.

The Journey Begins

On October 15, 1997, the National Aeronautics and [3] Space Administration (NASA) launched the Cassini-Huygens spacecraft at Cape Canaveral, Florida. This mission was no ordinary launch. The massive spacecraft was too heavy to launch directly to Saturn. It did not have enough power to reach Saturn's orbit by itself. Instead, scientists used three planets to help. How can planets offer assistance?

End-of-Unit Assessment • Unit 3 continued

Scientists used a method called gravity assist, or "fly-by." During a fly-by, a spacecraft flies by a planet. The planet's gravity tugs on the spacecraft. The spacecraft pulls away from the planet. However, the planet's gravity pulls it back again. The force created by the back and forth motion gives the spacecraft extra power. The spacecraft moves father away from the planet each time it pulls back. Finally, the spacecraft is able to pull away completely from the planet. The spacecraft then travels deeper into space with its extra power.

4

In April 1998, Cassini and Huygens did a fly-by near Venus. A little more than a year later, the spacecraft orbited Venus again. A few months later, the spacecraft circled Earth in a third fly-by. Cassini and Huygens finally had enough energy to leave the inner solar system. In December 2000, the spacecraft received its fourth and final gravity assist when it flew by Jupiter. Cassini and Huygens were on their way to Saturn!

5

On Christmas Eve 2004, Cassini and Huygens separated for the first time. They had traveled more than 2 billion miles together. Now each probe would perform its special function. Cassini's job was to take photos and collect data on Saturn's rings and moons. It would circle the planet for 4 years. Huygens's task was to land on Titan's surface, using a parachute. After landing, it would collect data.

6

Solid or Liquid?

What did scientists hope Huygens might find on Titan? Where would the probe land? Would Huygens land on solid ground? Would it splash down in liquid? Scientists speculated that Titan might be covered with lakes and oceans. Because Titan has extremely strong winds, scientists expected the liquid to have choppy waves.

7

If Huygens landed in a liquid, it would sink after a few moments. Still, scientists thought pictures could be taken within the liquid and sent back to Earth. After all, Huygens's specialized tools were good for studying liquids. On the other hand, if the probe landed on a solid surface, it would last longer and take more pictures.

8

End-of-Unit Assessment • Unit 3 continued

However, if the probe fell or broke on the hard surface, then collected data might be lost. On January 14, 2005, Huygens landed solidly on Titan's misty, frozen ground.

Although they are no longer connected, the two space probes are working together. Huygens's pictures and data from Titan's surface are sent to Cassini. Cassini then transmits the findings to Earth.   9

Fascinating Findings

What has Huygens found? One of its first discoveries was that Titan's surface is frozen solid. The surface is similar to frozen sand or clay. In fact, the Celsius temperature is about 180 degrees below zero (about −292 degrees Fahrenheit), which is much colder than the freezing point of water on Earth.   10

Pictures from Huygens gave scientists other valuable information. Titan's surface looks much like a shore covered with pebble-shaped objects. Data also show that clouds of gas contain a substance called methane. Scientists are excited by this information because methane is associated with forms of life. Scientists are wondering where the methane comes from. Could there be a form of life on Titan?   11

In many ways, Titan resembles Earth. It has hills and flat areas. It also appears to have a network of river and lake beds, but they are currently dry.   12

Evidence from Huygens suggests that the weather patterns on Titan can change. Does Titan have a rainy season? Is it possible that rain fills up the riverbeds and later the beds dry up? Scientists do not have the answers, but thanks to Cassini and Huygens, they are learning more about Titan each day.   13

End-of-Unit Assessment • Unit 3 continued

Circle the letter of the correct answer to each question.

1. Which of these does the author use in paragraph 1 to lead readers to predict that the two travelers are on a mission?

   a. *soar through space*

   b. *dodge asteroids and ice*

   c. *make it to their target safely*

2. Which of the following predictions for the entire passage has been elaborated?

   a. A set of twins go on vacation together.

   b. Twins travel somewhere, find out whether something is solid or liquid, and find out interesting things.

   c. Twins are born, separated at birth, and then find each other.

3. Why did scientists use the "fly-by" method to send Cassini and Huygens to Saturn?

   a. because the space probes needed to stay attached to each other

   b. because the probes were too heavy to launch directly to Saturn

   c. because the "fly-by" method would get them to Saturn quicker than any other way of flying

4. What causes a planet and a spacecraft to pull back and forth on each other?

   a. gravity

   b. Saturn

   c. stars

5. Which of the following findings best supports the prediction that Titan might have forms of life?

   a. deltas

   b. methane

   c. wind

End-of-Unit Assessment · Unit 3 continued

6. Which of the following predictions based on the subhead "Solid or Liquid?" has been elaborated?

   a. The probes will find that the surface of Titan is solid.

   b. The probes will find that the surface of Titan is a liquid.

   c. The probes will identify something as a solid or a liquid.

7. What do the temperature findings on Titan confirm?

   a. Titan has a frozen surface.

   b. Titan has forms of life.

   c. Titan has the same temperature as Earth.

8. According to paragraphs 10 and 11, which of the following is the surface of Titan most like?

   a. dark rain forest

   b. cold beach

   c. hot desert

9. Which of the following is a good prediction of what would most likely happen if Cassini breaks down in space?

   a. Huygens would not collect data.

   b. Titan would have no data to collect.

   c. Earth would not receive data.

10. What should you do if the prediction you have made doesn't match what you read?

    a. You should change your prediction.

    b. Read the entire passage before changing your prediction.

    c. Don't make any more predictions.

End-of-Unit Assessment • Unit 3 continued

Part 3 Fluency

Read the following passage once. Then read it again as your teacher times you. Underline the word you are reading when your teacher says to stop. Then answer the question.

The powered-down ship now had oxygen coming from the lunar module *Aquarius*. But, it was freezing. The astronauts' clothes and sleeping bags were designed for sleeping in a warm ship. Haise shivered and listened to his crewmates shouting back and forth with Mission Control. He was supposed to rest for 6 hours, but he gave up after 2. Then, he floated back to *Aquarius*.

Lovell was feeling the strain. The Moon was now less than 40,000 miles away. Looking at the Moon through a porthole window, Lovell told Haise, "I'm afraid this is going to be the last Moon mission for a long time." He didn't intend the comment to reflect poorly on the space program. Unfortunately, reporters picked up on the remark over a microphone system. They passed it on to a public eager for news of *Apollo 13*.

People around the world were following the news story anxiously. Superstitious people pointed to the fact that the unlucky mission was named Apollo 13. The spacecraft had also left Houston at 2:13 p.m. The number 13 has traditionally been associated with bad luck. The astronauts, however, were so busy trying to survive that they were not aware they had captured the attention of the world.

Which of the following is the prediction that Lovell makes?

a. The Apollo 13 mission will reach the Moon soon.

b. The Apollo 13 mission will be the last moon mission for a long time.

c. The Apollo 13 mission will fail because of the unlucky number 13.

Mid-Unit Assessment
Unit 4

Part 1 Vocabulary

Circle *a* or *b* to answer each question.

WORD LIST

abruptly

agreement

chaos

commercial

deliberately

disastrous

distorted

enthusiasm

glamorous

humiliation

intrigued

overcrowded

probably

realistic

transforming

uncertainty

1. Is a *distorted* story all true?

   a. yes   **b.** no

2. If an experience is *transforming*, does it change you?

   a. yes   **b.** no

3. Is it *disastrous* when everyone feels prepared for a test?

   a. yes   **b.** no

4. Is a fairy tale usually *realistic*?

   a. yes   **b.** no

5. Is the purpose of a *commercial* usually to sell something?

   a. yes   **b.** no

Circle the letter of the word that best completes each sentence.

6. Marc's _____ about the time could be the reason why he showed up an hour early.

   a. chaos   **b.** uncertainty   **c.** humiliation

7. Some people _____ plan all of the steps before beginning a project.

   a. realistic   **b.** intrigued   **c.** deliberately

8. The _____ in the room caused everyone to worry.

   a. distorted   **b.** chaos   **c.** glamorous

Mid-Unit Assessment · Unit 4 continued

9. I thought that the room was _____ with furniture.

    a. probably   **b.** uncertainty   **c.** overcrowded

10. Everyone at the meeting came to an _____ about the best course of action.

    a. agreement   **b.** abruptly   **c.** enthusiasm

11. Many people believe that famous people lead _____ lives.

    a. glamorous   **b.** agreement   **c.** chaos

Circle the letter of the form of the word that best completes each sentence.

12. The woman stopped _____ when she suddenly realized she had forgotten her keys.

    a. abruptly   **b.** abrupt

13. Max couldn't forget the _____ of tripping and falling in the cafeteria.

    a. humble   **b.** humiliation

14. I am _____ about trying out for the team.

    a. enthusiasm   **b.** enthusiastic

15. The clouds in the sky indicate that it will _____ rain.

    a. probable   **b.** probably

Mid-Unit Assessment • Unit 4 continued

Part 2 Comprehension: Text Structure

Read the passage and answer the questions at the end of the passage.

The Real Deal

The television camera provides a sweeping view of
San Diego Bay as a popular song begins to play. One boat's
red sails stand out against a mass of white boats in the
overcrowded harbor. Abruptly, the camera settles on the
deck of a house overlooking the harbor. The house is
painted bright blue. The color is only a few shades deeper
than the cloudless California sky. Five housemates sit
around a patio table, talking and laughing. A large white
umbrella protects them from the sun. Two others play pool
at the far end of the deck. They're all in their late teens or
early twenties. 1

Sound familiar? The setting is season 14 of *The
Real World*, a long-running reality TV show. Each year the
glamorous settings and housemates change. The plot
remains the same, though. Seven strangers live together
under the watchful eyes of a film crew. 2

When *The Real World* first aired on television in 1992,
many viewers were intrigued. Where else could you see
ordinary people live out their daily lives in front of cameras?
The show's plot and setting were original. However, the idea
of tracking the lives of ordinary people through the lens of a
television camera was not. Reality television already had a
rich history. 3

The Up Series

One of the first attempts to use television cameras
to track the lives of ordinary people occurred in Great
Britain. In 1963, a television crew filmed 14 girls and boys,
all aged seven. The children lived in different places in
Great Britain and came from a variety of backgrounds. They
were asked about their daily lives. They were also asked
what they hoped to do in the future. Their stories aired on
British television the next year as *Seven Up*. 4

Mid-Unit Assessment • Unit 4 continued

Seven Up was originally meant to be a one-time project. **5**
However, a crewmember thought that it would be interesting
to track the children's lives over time. As a result, the *Up*
series was born. However, the series was far from a weekly
show. The second show aired seven years after the first
show. The second show was called *7 Plus Seven*. It
followed the same children who were now age 14. This
show was followed in seven more years by *21 Up*. Since
that time, most of the original 14 people have agreed to
appear on camera every seven years. The latest show was
filmed in 2005. It was the seventh show in the series. In
49 Up, the kids were 49 years old.

An American Family

The next big step in the development of reality TV **6**
occurred in the United States. In 1971, filmmakers
asked the Loud family from California to participate in
a television series about an American family. Originally,
the Louds were supposed to be one of four families whose
lives would be filmed. The Louds would represent the
West Coast. The other families would be chosen from
the Midwest, the South, and the East Coast. Each family
would be filmed for four weeks.

Once the project was well underway, the Louds were told **7**
that they were the only family being filmed. Instead of four
weeks of filming, the crew filmed for seven months. In
many ways, the experience was disastrous for the Louds.
Among the things that the cameras captured was the
breakup of Pat and Bill Loud's marriage. When *An American
Family* finally aired in 1973, more than 10 million viewers
watched the marriage fall apart week by week.

Ten years later, the filmmakers aired an update. It was **8**
called *An American Family Revisited*. In the update, Pat and
Bill Loud and their children talked about the original series.
They also talked about their lives afterward. For Pat Loud,
the original series was a humiliation. Too many people had
watched the breakup of her marriage and other private
details about her family.

Mid-Unit Assessment · Unit 4 continued

Is <u>The Real World</u> the Real Deal?

An American Family is often credited with launching reality television in the United States. Television couldn't get much more realistic than the Louds. Can the same be said for *The Real World*? How does it fit into the history of reality TV? 9

Like *An American Family*, *The Real World* films the daily lives of ordinary people. However, the reality of that life is a bit distorted. The house is more like a television set than a home. In San Diego, for example, a former restaurant was temporarily transformed into a house. And what about the people living together in the house? The seven strangers are picked from thousands of applicants. The show's producers make their choices with the hope of creating exciting television. This decision often means choosing a mix of people that will create a little conflict and chaos. 10

The mix of reality and fiction leads some people to say that *The Real World* has done more than build on past forms of reality TV. Instead, they say, it has taken reality TV in a new direction. Many people credit the program with paving the way for other popular reality TV shows such as *Survivor* and *The Amazing Race*. 11

Does the audience feel that the shows represent real life? To many people it doesn't matter. In fact, reality television shows are among the most popular shows watched by viewers. New television lineups include even more programs focused on reality shows. These shows include competitions in surviving different hostile settings. These setting including far-away jungles, the business world, and even golf courses. TV watchers have been fascinated with the real-life approach to entertainment for years. Many television producers are betting that TV audiences will continue to do so. 12

Mid-Unit Assessment • Unit 4 continued

Circle the letter of the correct answer to each question.

1. Which of the following could you tell about the passage by previewing it?

   a. The passage probably describes a family that claims to be American but really isn't.

   b. The passage probably describes some television shows featuring real people.

   c. The passage probably describes people who like to watch TV shows filmed in San Diego, California.

2. Why does knowing the text structures in a passage like "The Real Deal" help you to understand it?

   a. It helps me to identify the topic and the supporting details.

   b. It helps me understand the passage's organization.

   c. It helps me to use past experiences to better understand the passage.

3. What text structure is used in paragraphs 1 and 2?

   a. description

   b. sequence

   c. problem and solution

4. Which signal words help determine the text structure of paragraphs 1 and 2?

   a. *red sails, watchful eyes*

   b. *abruptly, each year*

   c. *sound familiar, long-running*

5. Which statement is NOT true about the show *The Real World*?

   a. It is the longest-running reality show.

   b. It first aired on television in 1992.

   c. The setting is the same each year.

Mid-Unit Assessment • Unit 4 continued

6. Which words in paragraph 5 signal sequence?

   a. *originally, after, first, latest*

   b. *one-time, track, born, since*

   c. *meant, weekly, aired, followed*

7. How can you determine that the section "An American Family" is a sequence text structure?

   a. by reading the underlined words

   b. by reading the subhead

   c. by reading the first sentence of each paragraph

8. How did Pat Loud feel about appearing on *An American Family*?

   a. She was happy that her family was selected from among thousands of applicants.

   b. She was embarrassed that an audience witnessed her family's problems.

   c. She didn't like watching herself on TV, but she was glad to receive money for it.

9. Which program is credited for launching reality television programs in the United States?

   a. *The Real World*

   b. *Seven Up*

   c. *An American Family*

10. What text structure is used in the "Is The Real World the Real Deal?" section?

   a. problem and solution

   b. description

   c. sequence

Mid-Unit Assessment • Unit 4 continued

Part 3 Fluency

Read the following passage once. Then read it again as your teacher times you. Underline the word you are reading when your teacher says to stop. Then answer the question.

Carlos sat in bed thinking about what Robbie McMyers had said.
He wanted to air the show—or at least some of it—before the summer
schedule. Uncle Ricky was elated at this news, but Carlos could not
share his enthusiasm.

If that show went on before summer, all the kids at school would get
a good look at the lunacy and chaos going on in his family. He'd never
live it down and, what was worse, Alicia would never, ever agree to go
to the dance with him.

Sam jumped into his room, twirling his cape. "Which pose is better?"
he asked. He sucked in his cheeks and lifted his cape up to his chin.
Then he switched positions, throwing the cape back over his shoulders
and standing with his hands on his hips.

"I don't know," Carlos replied. "The first pose makes you look like
Dracula and the second one makes it seem as if you think you're
Superman."

"I'll use the first one then," Sam decided. "It fits my image better."

"Robbie just told us some good news," Sam added. "His network told
him that they can't air the show before summer."

"That is good news," Carlos said enthusiastically.

Which words show that the text structure of the paragraph is description?

a. *before the summer schedule*

b. *the kids at school would get a good look at the lunacy*

c. *twirling his cape*

End-of-Unit Assessment
Unit 4

Part 1 Vocabulary

Circle *a* or *b* to answer each question.

WORD LIST

accidental
animated
barrier
calculated
conflict
cooperative
exquisite
harmony
industrious
lofty
lure
management
obstacle
pose
torment
unison

1. Can two people sing a song in *unison*?

    a. yes   **b.** no

2. If people are *industrious*, are they lazy?

    a. yes   **b.** no

3. Can someone *pose* for a photographer?

    a. yes   **b.** no

4. Can *barriers* prevent you from entering a building?

    a. yes   **b.** no

5. Can a bird's nest be a *lofty* site?

    a. yes   **b.** no

Circle the letter of the word that best completes each sentence.

6. The bakery owner hoped that the smell of hot bread would _____ customers.

    a. pose   **b.** lure   **c.** unison

7. Sara knew that the project would be easier if everyone was _____.

    a. cooperative   **b.** calculated   **c.** exquisite

8. Everyone became _____ when the star of the show came out to give autographs.

    a. posed   **b.** accidental   **c.** animated

9. The design on the front of the jacket was _____.

    a. exquisite   **b.** lofty   **c.** management

End-of-Unit Assessment • Unit 4 continued

10. His every action seemed _____ to bring about
laughter in the audience.

    a. lure   **b.** calculated   **c.** cooperative

11. Although he made it look _____, Ray had carefully
planned sitting next to Jessica.

    a. accidental   **b.** lofty   **c.** industrious

12. It is peaceful when people live in _____ with each
other.

    a. conflict   **b.** torment   **c.** harmony

13. I knew that good project _____ was key to
completing my task on time.

    a. barriers   **b.** obstacles   **c.** management

14. Andy was _____ by what he'd said to his friend
in anger.

    a. tormented   **b.** lofty   **c.** cooperative

15. Fallen rocks are an _____ you can face when hiking.

    a. unison   **b.** accidental   **c.** obstacle

End-of-Unit Assessment • Unit 4 continued

Part 2 Comprehension: Text Structure

Read the passage and answer the questions at the end of
the passage.

Early Hip-Hop

In the 1970s, a new trend started in some 1
neighborhoods of the South Bronx in New York City.
This trend was called hip-hop. Early hip-hop culture
was a blend of music, dance, art, and dress.

Hip-hop developed partly as a reaction to disco music. 2
Disco was the most popular form of dance music at the
time. People crowded into clubs to dance to disco's strong
beat. Over time, however, some people became bored
with it. They argued that as the popularity of disco spread
around the world, the music lost its edge. For people in
the South Bronx, hip-hop was the response.

Hip-Hop Versus Disco

Early hip-hop and disco shared some traits. Both had 3
roots in African-American and Latin music. Both also
started in New York City. In addition, both relied on
disc jockeys, or DJs, to play records for a crowd. The
similarities ended there, however. Disco was a money-
making business. Hip-hop was music born on the streets.

Record companies spent millions of dollars to create 4
and market disco music. Business people calculated what
it would take to lure record buyers. Producers recorded and
rerecorded musicians and singers. They mixed and remixed
recordings until they thought the sound was just right. The
process was much different in hip-hop. The producers of
early hip-hop didn't rely on musicians in recording studios.
Instead, they created music out of bits and pieces of
recordings that already existed. They needed only two
turntables, some records, a power source, and a big dose
of creativity.

The role of DJs also differed between disco and hip-hop. **5** Disco DJs simply played records and entertained a dance crowd. However, early hip-hop DJs produced live music by using their records and turntables as instruments. They jumped within and between records to capture sounds and bits of lyrics. They added to the effect by using the turntable needle to scratch the records. Scratching required quickly moving records back and forth under the needle.

DJs also worked in different places. Disco DJs worked **6** in dance clubs. People usually had to pay to get into these clubs. Hip-hop DJs, on the other hand, could set up shop anywhere where they could find a power supply. A street corner, playground, or basketball court could be instantly transformed into a free outdoor dance club.

Hip-Hop Culture

From the beginning, hip-hop was more than just music. **7** It was a culture. This culture was directly shaped by African-American and Latin traditions as well as by the realities of life in the South Bronx.

Rather than being a barrier to creating hip-hop culture, a **8** lack of money helped shape it. Early hip-hoppers couldn't afford to buy expensive musical instruments or rent time in recording studies. Thus, they created music out of records that already existed.

Many young people also couldn't afford to buy tickets **9** to dance clubs. As a result, hip-hoppers took their music and culture to public areas. This openness increased the number of people exposed to hip-hop music. These people, in turn, helped the culture to grow and change. Break dancing, for instance, became a street expression of hip-hop. This type of dance involved athletic movements and spinning on the head and shoulders. Learning the moves didn't require money. Anyone industrious enough to learn the moves could draw a crowd and show off his or her skills.

End-of-Unit Assessment • Unit 4 continued

Other elements of hip-hop grew out of earlier traditions   10
or practices. DJs wanted to generate excitement at their
performances. To help animate the crowd, they worked
with performers called MCs (masters of ceremonies) who
rhymed lyrics over the music. This rhyming came to be
called rapping. Rapping owed much to the street game of
Dozens and the practice of Jamaican toasting. In Dozens,
people trade complicated fake insults until one person
gives in. Jamaican toasting involves chanting or talking
during a song. Rap drew from these traditions and
eventually became the central focus of hip-hop.

Similarly, hip-hop art grew out of tagging. In tagging,   11
a person spray paints his or her initials or nickname in
public places. It is usually illegal to spray paint on public
property. As a result, the practice often led to conflicts
between hip-hoppers and police officers. Some talented
taggers, however, received permission to create murals on
buildings and walls.

From the Street to Mainstream

In the beginning, hip-hop DJs created their music live.   12
This practice limited the spread of hip-hop to the streets
of large cities. However, hip-hoppers eventually began to
record their tunes. These recordings led to the first two rap
songs hitting the pop charts in 1979.

As more hip-hoppers recorded their songs, hip-hop   13
record labels grew. Large record labels also started to sign
hip-hop artists. As the market for hip-hop spread, even hip-
hop movies began to appear. Movies like *Breakin'* and *Beat
Street*, which were released in 1984, introduced hip-hop
culture to a wider audience. Hip-hop was on its way.

Circle the letter of the correct answer to each question.

1. Which of the following was NOT a part of hip-hop
culture?

a. dance

b. art

c. sports

End-of-Unit Assessment • Unit 4 continued

2. What was the cause of the development of hip-hop?

   a. Dance clubs were overcrowded.

   b. Some people became bored with disco.

   c. Disco was not a money-making business.

3. Which is the main kind of text structure used in the "Hip-Hop Versus Disco" section?

   a. fact and opinion

   b. compare and contrast

   c. cause and effect

4. Which of the following is one way in which hip-hop differs from disco?

   a. Hip-hop is created from existing music.

   b. Hip-hop requires a DJ and a power supply.

   c. Hip-hop has roots in African-American and Latin music.

5. Which of the following is true for both hip-hop and disco?

   a. Both disco and hip-hop used DJs.

   b. Disco and hip-hop dancers spun on their heads.

   c. Both disco and hip-hop were developed in the South Bronx.

6. Which of the following was affected by the practice of Jamaican toasting?

   a. break dancing

   b. tagging

   c. rap music

End-of-Unit Assessment • Unit 4 continued

7. Which of the following is an opinion?

   a. As disco spread around the world, the music lost its edge.

   b. As more hip-hoppers recorded their songs, hip-hop record labels grew.

   c. Rapping owed much to the practice of Jamaican toasting and the street game of Dozens.

8. Which signal words tell you that the section "From the Street to Mainstream" has a sequence text structure?

   a. *In the beginning, started to, began*

   h. *created, spread, appear*

   c. *practice, record, sign*

9. Why did tagging cause conflicts?

   a. Because DJs used tagging to promote disco and not hip-hop.

   b. Because spraying paint on public places is usually illegal.

   c. Because tagging requires people to insult each other.

10. Which is the best summary of this passage?

   a. Hip-hop developed as a reaction to disco music. There are many similarities between hip-hop and disco, as well as many differences. A lack of money helped shape hip-hop's development. Hip-hop eventually became very popular.

   b. Disco was a popular form of music played in dance clubs. It was a huge-money making business. DJs played disco music to increase its popularity. Disco has its roots in African-American and Latin music.

   c. DJs are the most important people in the music industry. They play music in dance clubs and out on streets. DJs helped establish disco music and hip-hop culture. DJs invented scratching by using a turntable and a needle.

End-of-Unit Assessment • Unit 4 continued

Part 3 Fluency

Read the following passage once. Then read it again as your teacher times you. Underline the word you are reading when your teacher says to stop. Then answer the question.

Before you think about recording and sending your music to record
companies, you should know a few things about how record companies
work. Record companies are also called record labels. There are many
different kinds of record labels. For example, some companies record
hip-hop, others record rock, and others record country music. It is
important to locate the right kinds of labels for your music. The company
and its bands have to work in harmony—they have to have the same goals.

A label's distribution is very important. The distribution is how
many copies of a CD a record label makes and where it sends them.
Labels vary widely. Some labels print 1,000 copies of a CD. Some print
1,000,000. Some labels put copies of their CDs only in local stores in
their city. Other labels send copies to every record store in the world.
Some small labels are happy if their band sells 20,000 CDs. Major labels
are disappointed if a band doesn't sell 500,000 CDs! A band must see
eye to eye with the record label about distribution.

All bands want to sell lots of CDs, and they are willing to do whatever
it takes to meet this goal. Sometimes meeting this goal means that a band
has to deliberately change its sound to sell more CDs.

Which text structure does the author use when talking about
different record labels?

a. sequence

b. problem and solution

c. compare and contrast

Mid-Unit Assessment
Unit 5

Part 1 Vocabulary

Circle *a* or *b* to answer each question.

WORD LIST

ambition

collision

decline

efficient

enable

function

hazard

hypothesize

maximum

overwhelming

perceive

precaution

precise

restraint

variation

visualize

1. Is fighting crime a *function* of a police department?

   a. yes   **b.** no

2. Does a scientist *hypothesize* before performing an experiment?

   a. yes   **b.** no

3. When you *visualize* an ocean, are you actually swimming in it?

   a. yes   **b.** no

4. Is an icy bridge a *hazard* to drivers?

   a. yes   **b.** no

Circle the letter of the word that best completes each sentence.

5. Doing two things at one time may not be an _____ way to get things done.

   a. enable   **b.** efficient   **c.** overwhelming

6. My _____ is to go to medical school and become a doctor.

   a. precaution   **b.** maximum   **c.** ambition

7. Julio's excellent grades _____ him to make the honor roll.

   a. restraint   **b.** enabled   **c.** hypothesized

8. Our cat seems to know the _____ moment that she will be fed.

   a. precise   **b.** maximum   **c.** overwhelming

Mid-Unit Assessment • Unit 5 continued

9. That new song is a _____ of an old song.

    a. restraint   **b.** function   **c.** variation

10. The _____ aroma of the lasagna in the oven made me hungry!

    a. efficient   **b.** declined   **c.** overwhelming

11. The _____ amount of books the shelf can hold is ten.

    a. function   **b.** hazard   **c.** maximum

Circle the letter of the word that has almost the same meaning as the underlined word.

12. Sue <u>noticed</u> that people were getting restless waiting for the show to begin.

    a. enabled   **b.** perceived   **c.** declined

13. We set our alarm system each night as a <u>protection</u> against burglars.

    a. precaution   **b.** hazard   **c.** collision

14. The driver was not hurt in the <u>accident</u> because he was wearing his seat belt.

    a. collision   **b.** variation   **c.** restraint

15. The calmer winds indicated that the storm had <u>weakened</u>.

    a. enabled   **b.** declined   **c.** visualized

Mid-Unit Assessment • Unit 5 continued

Part 2 Comprehension: Visualizing

Read the passage and answer the questions at the end of the passage.

Racing School

Did you ever watch a car race and wonder where the drivers learned their skills? Chances are they went to racing school!   1

At racing school, qualified instructors turn students into expert drivers who can take hairpin turns at maximum speeds. Many famous race car drivers, such as Jeff Gordon and Kyle Petty, got their start at racing schools. Some Hollywood celebrities have attended racing schools, too.   2

Of course, an overwhelming number of students are not famous people. Whether famous or unknown, racing school students have one thing in common—they love driving at high speeds. Racing schools teach them the skills they need to drive safely at those speeds. Many students also achieve their goal of experiencing the exciting world of auto racing.   3

Getting Ready

You may wonder how a beginning race car student gets his or her start. Many people use the Internet as a starting point. They research different racing schools and read about students' experiences at the schools. Once you decide on a school, you must reserve a spot and pay the fee for a beginner class. A typical beginner class lasts from 1 to 3 days.   4

There are three important items you need to bring to   5
racing school—racing shoes, socks, and driving gloves.
Racing schools supply everything else you will need. They
give you the proper clothing to wear while you race,
including your helmet. Of course, they also provide the race
car that you will drive. Classroom instruction, textbooks,
and track time are all part of the class.

Start Your Engines

On your first day of racing school, your instructor   6
will teach you all about race cars, equipment, and race
tracks. Then comes the moment you've been waiting for—
climbing into a real formula race car! However, you're not
ready to send up clouds of exhaust into the air just yet. The
goal is to learn important skills such as braking and
downshifting gears. These skills will help you control
your speed. They can also help you avoid hazards and
collisions on the racetrack. After all, keeping control of your
car and your speed is the most important function
of race car driving.

The second day is spent learning drills in braking   7
and passing other cars. These drills are practiced during
lapping sessions. During a lapping session, you and other
student drivers will circle the track one lap at a time.
You will practice braking, passing, and shifting gears, while
increasing your speed to 150 miles per hour. Soon the
landscape will become a blur. Tires screech. The smell
of burning rubber will fill the air. You will feel cars whiz by
at amazing speeds. Every student driver has the same
goal—to be as fast as possible.

So where are the instructors? In the classroom,   8
they are easy to see. On the race course, it's a different
story. Instructors drive cars on the track, too. From their
cars, they can carefully watch you. At times, they race
around the track among the students, monitoring their
performance. After all, the instructors need to study your
driving at every angle. After each drive on the track,
instructors will give you feedback and suggestions.

Mid-Unit Assessment • Unit 5 continued

On the third day, it's time to race against others! You've been waiting for this competition. Double-file racing is the event. You and all the other student drivers get into your formula race cars and buckle up. Then, the race cars line up on the track two-by-two. Your heart beats wildly. You plan ways to grab hold of the lead and keep it at all costs. Engines roar as you and all the other racers wait for the signal. An instructor waves the green flag, and the race is officially started. Dozens of horse-powered cars take off in a fury. Lap after lap, you race at incredible speeds.

9

Going the Distance

Three exciting days have ended. You have successfully graduated from a beginning race car class. What happens next? For some people, a goal has been met. They are satisfied and go home with smiles on their faces. For others, this is just the beginning. Many graduates apply for a regional Sports Car Club of America (SCCA) competition license. This license enables racers to compete in road racing. Other graduates go on to train at intermediate- and advanced-level race courses. They strive to improve their road performance. These race drivers look for every competitive edge.

10

Whether you take one racing school course or many of them, race car driving is an exciting experience. The roar of an engine and the shifting of gears will have your heart racing almost as fast as your car!

11

Circle the letter of the correct answer to each question.

1. Which of the following explains why people use the Internet to learn about racing schools?

a. It helps them to decide which racing school to attend.

b. They can apply for a Sports Car Club of America license.

c. They can find out which racing schools have trained Hollywood celebrities.

Mid-Unit Assessment • Unit 5 continued

2. How does the picture help you understand what you read?

   a. The picture shows that people who learn to drive race cars become Hollywood celebrities.

   b. The picture shows that student race car drivers wear safety equipment and get to drive real formula race cars.

   c. The picture shows that students at racing schools become qualified professional race car drivers.

3. Why are learning to brake and to downshift gears important driving skills?

   a. They help you control your speed.

   b. They help you to drive at maximum speed.

   c. They help you to pass other cars during a race.

4. In paragraph 7, what does the descriptive phrase "the landscape will become a blur" help you visualize?

   a. students learning to brake

   b. drivers feeling tired

   c. driving at maximum speed

5. In paragraph 7, which sensory words help you visualize race car driving?

   a. *learning* and *practice*

   b. *drills* and *shifting gears*

   c. *screech* and *smell of burning rubber*

6. Why do instructors drive on the racetrack?

   a. to monitor their students' performance and give them feedback

   b. to race against their students to give their students more experience

   c. to show their students their skills as race car drivers

Mid-Unit Assessment • Unit 5 continued

7. In paragraph 9, which description helps you visualize the excitement of racing?

   a. *On the third day, it's time to race against others!*

   b. *Double-file racing is the event.*

   c. *Your heart beats wildly.*

8. Why do people who graduate from racing school apply for a Sports Car Club of America competition license?

   a. to show that they have successfully completed racing school

   b. to compete in road races

   c. to be able to train on intermediate- and advanced-level race courses

9. Which of the following is the correct sequence of events at racing school?

   a. You learn drills in braking and passing other cars; you learn about race cars, equipment, and racetracks; you race against others.

   b. You race against others, you learn drills in braking and passing other cars; you learn about race cars, equipment, and racetracks.

   c. You learn about race cars, equipment, and racetracks; you learn drills in braking and passing; you race against others.

10. Which do you think is the best conclusion to draw from this passage?

   a. Students who attend racing school learn how dangerous race car driving is.

   b. Students who attend racing school satisfy their goal of learning to drive real race cars.

   c. Students who have attended racing school go on to win professional competitions.

Mid-Unit Assessment • Unit 5 continued

Part 3 Fluency

Read the following passage once. Then read it again as your teacher times you. Underline the word you are reading when your teacher says to stop. Then answer the question.

Imagine two people, living in different countries, who had never
met having the same idea at the same time. This is how the jet
engine came to be. A British Royal Air Force officer worked in
England, while a German engineer worked in Germany. Each man
produced a jet engine. They both created internal combustion
engines, which meant that airplanes could fly without propellers.

An internal combustion engine needs air to work. A jet engine
uses fans to suck in air. As the air collides with the fuel, an electric
spark causes an explosion. Burning fuel shoots out of the back of the
engine. As the flames of gas shoot back, they thrust the jet engine
(and the airplane) forward.

The German jet engine flew first. On August 27, 1939, Heinkel
He-178 became the first jet-powered flight in history. A week later,
World War II began. Countries needed to use airplanes for combat.
The German air force became the first to use the jet engine in a
fighter plane. The first jet fighter had two jet engines and could fly
540 mph! After the war, airline companies began to fly airplanes
with jet engines.

Which paragraph helps you visualize how a jet engine works?

a. the first paragraph

b. the second paragraph

c. the third paragraph

End-of-Unit Assessment
Unit 5

Part 1 Vocabulary

Circle *a* or *b* to answer each question.

WORD LIST

abundant

conceal

contour

contribute

decade

decay

design

durable

incomplete

ingenious

intricate

monumental

necessity

phase

specifications

sufficient

1. If you skip a few math problems, is your math homework *incomplete*?

   a. yes   **b.** no

2. Should *durable* shoes need to be replaced often?

   a. yes   **b.** no

3. Does a rotting log *decay*?

   a. yes   **b.** no

4. If you leave for a moment, are you gone for a *decade*?

   a. yes   **b.** no

Circle the letter of the word that best completes each sentence.

5. The _____ of the dress was revealed at the fashion show.

   a. design   **b.** phase   **c.** intricate

6. Plants need a _____ amount of water to grow.

   a. durable   **b.** sufficient   **c.** contour

7. We _____ our time to volunteer at the children's hospital.

   a. necessity   **b.** contribute   **c.** phase

8. The team built the race car according to exact _____.

   a. contour   **b.** sufficient   **c.** specifications

End-of-Unit Assessment • Unit 5 continued

9. Our teacher said the planning _____ of the project should take up to 3 weeks.

    a. decade   **b.** phase   **c.** monumental

10. The _____ of the land is affected by its closeness to the shore.

    a. contour   **b.** phase   **c.** decade

11. The Civil War was a _____ event in American history.

    a. design   **b.** necessity   **c.** monumental

Circle the letter of the word that has the opposite meaning of the underlined word in each sentence.

12. The brilliant scientist planned the most <u>unoriginal</u> experiment.

    a. abundant   **b.** contour   **c.** ingenious

13. I tried to <u>reveal</u> my disappointment when Anwar said he was moving away.

    a. design   **b.** conceal   **c.** durable

14. The garden looked healthy because the tomatoes were <u>few</u>.

    a. abundant   **b.** intricate   **c.** contributed

15. Food and clothing are <u>luxuries</u> that all people must have.

    a. decades   **b.** phases   **c.** necessities

End-of-Unit Assessment • Unit 5 continued

Part 2 Comprehension: Visualizing

Read the passage and answer the questions at the end of the passage.

Bridges on the Move

Enemy foot soldiers invade like a colony of raging ants. Swords glisten in the sunlight. The soldiers' feet stomp on the ground as they draw closer to the castle. They are ready to overthrow the king. Just then, heavy chains pull up a clever device, leaving a treacherous moat between the enemy soldiers and the castle. The soldiers cannot get across. The king and his people are safely concealed within the castle. An ingenious device called a drawbridge has saved the kingdom.   1

For thousands of years, drawbridges protected castles against intruders. Today, drawbridges serve a different purpose. They are usually located over a body of water. Their moving parts allow tall vessels in the water beneath them to pass through. The moving parts classify a drawbridge as a movable bridge.   2

Two other kinds of bridges are similar to a drawbridge: the vertical lift bridge and the swing bridge. These bridges are also movable designs. Each of these bridges allows boats and ships to pass back and forth beneath them. Yet each type of movable bridge operates in a slightly different way.   3

How They Work

Drawbridges that protected castles were usually lifted by chains. The parts of modern drawbridges that lift are called spans. A span can be made up of two long, flat parts. When they are lowered, the parts meet end to end to create one long span. People travel across a span to get from one side of a bridge to the other side.   4

How do modern drawbridges work? Modern drawbridges use motors, gears, and counterweights. First, gears lift the two parts of the span where they meet in the center. Next, as the two parts of the spans are lifted, they also separate. Finally, counterweights apply pressure to the lowered ends of the span. The weights are needed to keep the lifted ends in the air. The way each piece of the span is lifted and kept in the air is similar to the way a seesaw works. In fact, drawbridges are commonly called bascule bridges. *Bascule* is a French word that means "seesaw."   5

Like drawbridges, vertical lift bridges also use motors, gears, and counterweights. However, they also use cables and pulleys. Vertical lift bridges have a one-piece span. Instead of the center of the span lifting and separating, pulleys and cables raise the entire span directly above the bridge. The span is raised high enough for water traffic to pass beneath it. Once boats have passed safely, the span is lowered to its original position.   6

A third type of movable bridge is the swing bridge. Its name describes exactly how it moves. The span can swing horizontally, back and forth over a body of water. A swing bridge works like a door opening and closing on its hinges. This type of movable bridge also uses motors and gears.   7

Problems to Solve

Although bridges are built to exact specifications, they can have limitations. Many of these limitations are not realized until after the bridges are built. For example, swing bridges operate more slowly than other kinds of movable bridges. As a result, many cities have replaced swing bridges with other kinds of bridges. Replacing them is quite expensive!   8

Vertical lift bridges and drawbridges have their problems, too. Vertical lift bridges must fight hard against the force of gravity. A typical vertical lift bridge raises its span high in the air more than 200 times a month. All of that weight lifting causes wear and tear on these bridges.   9

End-of-Unit Assessment • Unit 5 continued

Drawbridges also fight against gravity, perhaps even more so than vertical lift bridges. A drawbridge needs counterweights that are two to three times heavier than each piece of the span. A vertical lift bridge only needs a counterweight equal to the exact weight of the span.   10

Earthquake Challenges

Perhaps the bridges with the most challenging problems are the ones located in earthquake-prone areas. There is certainly no such thing as an "earthquake-proof" bridge. However, movable bridges can be made stronger and more resistant to the stress that an earthquake causes. Bridge columns can be reinforced with steel. Devices can be added to decrease the amount of bridge movement that occurs during an earthquake. Steel tie-down rods are also used to better anchor bridges to the ground. Bridges in earthquake-prone areas are built to be as stable as possible.   11

Circle the letter of the correct answer to each question.

1. In paragraph 1, which descriptive words help you visualize the soldiers as ants?

   a. *invade like a colony*

   b. *feet stomp on the ground*

   c. *swords glisten*

2. Why are movable bridges useful today?

   a. They protect a city against intruding ships.

   b. They allow water traffic to pass beneath them.

   c. They are not at all affected by earthquakes.

End-of-Unit Assessment • Unit 5 continued

3. According to paragraph 5, which is the first step in how a modern drawbridge works?

   a. Gears lift the two spans where they meet in the center.

   b. The two parts of the spans separate and lift in the air.

   c. Counterweights apply pressure to the lowered ends of the span.

4. Using the sequence of events in paragraph 5, which is the final image you created?

   a. people traveling across a bridge span getting from one side to the other

   b. two parts of a bridge span that are separated; one end of each part is lifted in the air

   c. a tall ship passing under a bridge span that is lifted high into the air

5. Why is a drawbridge called a bascule bridge?

   a. It uses counterweights called bascules.

   b. *Bascule* is the French word for "seesaw."

   c. The French built the first drawbridge.

6. Which would you see if you saw a vertical lift bridge working?

   a. The entire span lifted directly above the bridge.

   b. The bridge swinging out across a body of water.

   c. The two parts of the span lifting at the center and separating.

7. Which of the following helps you visualize how a swing bridge works?

   a. a seesaw

   b. a door opening and closing

   c. counterweights, pulleys, and cables

End-of-Unit Assessment • Unit 5 continued

VENN DIAGRAM

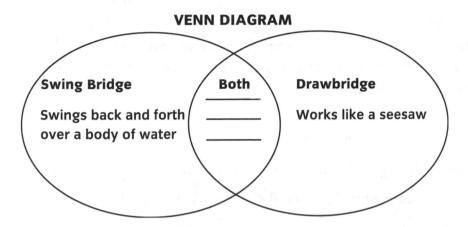

8. Which of the following belongs in the center of
the Venn diagram above?

a. Used to protect castles

b. Move slowly

c. Use motors and gears

9. How do the descriptive words *door opening and closing
on its hinges* and *seesaw* help a reader to understand
the text?

a. They help readers to visualize the activities people
often perform on a bridge.

b. They help readers to visualize the equipment used to
build a bridge.

c. They help readers to visualize and contrast the
different types of bridges.

10. Which is the effect of reinforcing bridge columns
with steel?

a. Steel makes bridges stronger and more resistant to the
stresses of earthquakes.

b. Steel decreases the amount of bridge movement that
occurs during an earthquake.

c. Steel is used as counterweight to help lift the span of
a drawbridge.

End-of-Unit Assessment • Unit 5 continued

Part 3 Fluency

Read the following passage once. Then read it again as your teacher times you. Underline the word you are reading when your teacher says to stop. Then answer the question.

One infamous bridge disaster occurred on December 28, 1879, in
Queensferry, Scotland. During a violent thunderstorm, a passenger train
rumbled onto the Tay Bridge, which crossed the Firth Bay of Tay. Just
then, the bridge buckled and collapsed. More than 70 passengers fell to a
watery death. Investigators never identified the main cause of the disaster.

On January 10, 1889, disaster struck the Falls View Suspension Bridge
that connected New York State and Canada near Niagara Falls. A terrible
storm raged the night before the disaster. Ferocious winds broke a
fastening on the bridge. Finally, the bridge tore away and fell into the
gorge below.

One of the worst bridge disasters on record occurred in fairly recent
times. On May 9, 1980, a blinding thunderstorm hit Tampa Bay, Florida.
A freight ship called the *Summit Venture* plowed into the 4-mile-long
Sunshine Skyway Bridge. The ship's crew did not see the bridge because it
was concealed by rain. A long section of the bridge plunged into the bay.
Thirty-five people in cars and a bus fell from the bridge to their deaths.

Today, engineers know a great deal about forces that destroy bridges.
They can add reinforcements to bridges to brace them against the force of
the wind. They can also use devices to reduce destructive vibrations
caused by the wind.

Which descriptive words help you to visualize Tay Bridge?
a. *buckled* and *collapsed*
b. *violent* and *crossed*
c. *fell* and *identified*

Mid-Unit Assessment
Unit 6

Part 1 Vocabulary

Circle *a* or *b* to answer each question.

1. Is a *rival* someone who competes against you?

    a. yes   **b.** no

2. If you are *immersed* in a book, do you find the book interesting?

    a. yes   **b.** no

3. During a *crisis*, are people usually happy?

    a. yes   **b.** no

4. Does health *insurance* help pay medical bills?

    a. yes   **b.** no

Circle the letter of the word that best completes each sentence.

5. Readers were delighted and amused by the author's _____ story.

    a. imaginative **b.** absorbed   **c.** rival

6. I heard that my favorite singer is _____ coming to town to perform.

    a. destined   **b.** subtlety   **c.** supposedly

7. Lifting weights all summer will _____ Leah's muscles.

    a. immerse   **b.** regret   **c.** strengthen

8. The suspenseful movie kept the audience _____ from start to finish.

    a. absorbed   **b.** perpetual   **c.** insurance

WORD LIST

absorbed

crisis

destined

imaginative

immerse

implying

insurance

momentarily

noticeably

perpetual

persistence

regret

rival

strengthen

subtlety

supposedly

Mid-Unit Assessment • Unit 6 continued

9. Without saying it directly, the lawyer was _____ that the defendant was guilty.

    a. implying   **b.** subtlety   **c.** imaginative

Circle the letter of the form of the word that correctly completes each sentence.

10. The dog looked _____ better after it was bathed and brushed.

    a. notice   **b.** noticeably

11. If you _____ in studying hard, you will earn good grades.

    a. persist   **b.** persistence

12. Because of her stage fright, Jane _____ forgot her lines.

    a. moment   **b.** momentarily

Circle the letter of the word that means almost the same as the underlined word or words.

13. You may <u>rue</u> the fact that you stopped taking music lessons.

    a. regret   **b.** rival   **c.** strengthen

14. Martin's <u>indirectness</u> makes it hard to know if he actually answered any questions.

    a. implying   **b.** crisis   **c.** subtlety

15. It seems that we will have to deal with the <u>continual</u> heat for months.

    a. perpetual   **b.** immerse   **c.** destined

Mid-Unit Assessment • Unit 6 continued

Part 2 Comprehension: Inferencing

Read the passage and answer the questions at the
end of the passage.

The Trickster's Greatest Hit

No one ever called Daniel by his real name. Everyone   1
knew him as "the Trickster" because of his perpetual
practical jokes. Daniel loved his nickname and made a
point of living up to it. Not a week went by that he didn't
dream up a practical joke to play on someone.

Daniel staged many of his practical jokes in the school   2
cafeteria because he liked to "perform" in front of as many
witnesses as possible. One of his best stunts was the time
his friend Jamal finally got up the nerve to sit with Tanya
Simms. While Jamal was absorbed in conversation with
Tanya, Daniel snuck up behind him. Daniel took off his own
belt and slipped it through the loops of Jamal's pants.
Daniel then fastened the belt to Jamal's chair. When Jamal
stood up to leave, the chair went with him. He lost his
balance and crashed onto the table. The noise made
everyone turn to look just as Jamal stood up covered with
spaghetti sauce and chocolate pudding. The crowd hooted
with laughter, and the Trickster took a bow.

Daniel's favorite location for morning pranks was the   3
bus drop-off area at school, where most students waited in
the morning. One of his most ingenious tricks took place
there. He set up his friend Tony by sending him a letter that
was supposedly from Ms. Layton, the principal. Daniel typed
a message saying that Tony had been chosen to dress as
the school mascot and compete in a citywide competition.
The winner's school would receive a trophy. It explained
that a special bus would pick Tony up in the morning before
school to take him downtown for the contest judging.

Mid-Unit Assessment • Unit 6 continued

On the morning of the phony contest, Tony arrived at school dressed as a pirate, the school mascot. He wore a frilly shirt, knee britches, and a hat with a big feather. He also had a plastic parrot on his shoulder. The special bus never came. When the school buses started dropping off students, everyone pointed and snickered at Tony's outfit. Then the principal arrived. 　　　4

"Tony, you can't wear that costume to class," scolded Ms. Layton. "Call your parents and have them bring you some acceptable clothing." 　　　5

Everyone burst into laughter, and Tony turned red. That's when the Trickster stepped forward, and once again, took a bow. 　　　6

One day, Daniel decided to stage a prank for his biggest audience ever. His target would be Jesse Rios who was running for class president. Daniel knew most of the students would come to hear Jesse's campaign speech after school on Monday. 　　　7

On Sunday afternoon, Daniel prepared for the big moment. He poured a powdered cherry drink mix into a jug and added plenty of water. Then he grabbed some clear fishing line and a big plastic bucket from the garage and hurried to the school. 　　　8

Jesse was to give his speech in the outdoor courtyard. He would stand on the stage under the arbor, a wooden framework covered with ivy. Daniel climbed the arbor and crawled to the spot directly above the platform where Jesse would stand. He cleared away some ivy to make an opening for the bucket to pour through. Then he cut a length of fishing line long enough to reach the seats in the audience. He positioned the bucket and tied the fishing line to its handle. Finally, he emptied the jug of cherry drink into the bucket. The set-up was perfect! *I am, without a doubt, the master Trickster*, he thought as he headed home. 　　　9

On Monday afternoon, Daniel hurried to the courtyard. He picked up the end of the fishing line and took a seat near the arbor. The courtyard filled with students, and Jesse took his place on the platform. Suddenly, Daniel noticed that the platform had been moved two feet to the right. It was no longer directly under the bucket! 　　　10

Mid-Unit Assessment • Unit 6 continued

Daniel dropped the fishing line and hurried up on stage to speak to Jesse.

"Good luck on your speech," he said. "I noticed that the platform is out of place. I'll move it over so everyone can see you better." 11

"Whatever," said Jesse with a shrug. "It looks OK to me, though." 12

As Daniel dragged the platform into place, Ms. Layton walked by. She picked up the fishing line lying on the ground and gave it a tug. Instantly, the bucket tipped over. 13

Daniel was momentarily stunned as the cherry drink splashed down all over him. A split second later a roar of laughter from the audience snapped him back to reality. He'd become the target of his own prank! When he saw his former victims in the audience laughing harder than everyone else, Daniel wished he could crawl out of sight. 14

"Well, Daniel," said Ms. Layton laughing, "it seems the Trickster has gotten a dose of his own medicine." 15

Daniel looked down at the sticky red mess that covered him. "Yes, ma'am," he said with a sheepish grin. "I guess you could say my face is REALLY red." 16

At that, the audience laughed even harder. As Daniel took one last bow, he made a monumental decision. The Trickster was officially retired! 17

Circle the letter of the correct answer to each question.

1. Which is an inference that you can make based on the passage?

   a. Daniel plays jokes because he dislikes people.

   b. Daniel plays jokes as a way of getting attention.

   c. Daniel plays jokes to embarrass his teachers.

Mid-Unit Assessment • Unit 6 continued

2. Which phrases from the text help you make an inference about Jamal's feelings toward Tanya?

   a. *got up the nerve; absorbed in conversation*

   b. *stood up to leave; lost his balance*

   c. *covered with spaghetti sauce; hooted with laughter*

3. What can you infer about Jamal's reaction to Daniel's prank?

   a. Jamal thought it was really funny and didn't mind getting food all over his clothes.

   b. Jamal was embarrassed and mad at Daniel for having made him look foolish in front of Tanya.

   c. Jamal was grateful to Daniel because the prank made Tanya notice Jamal's good sense of humor.

4. What can you infer about Daniel's attitude toward playing practical jokes?

   a. It's the only way to keep bullies from picking on you.

   b. It's all just for a laugh and doesn't really hurt anyone.

   c. It's a way to let others enjoy being the center of attention.

5. How did Daniel get an audience for the joke he played on Tony?

   a. He staged the prank in the cafeteria during a crowded lunch hour.

   b. He passed the word around school so everyone would know where to go.

   c. His letter told Tony to wait where most students waited in the morning.

Mid-Unit Assessment • Unit 6 continued

6. How did Daniel plan to embarrass Jesse?

  a. He planned to cause a bucket of red juice to spill on Jesse during Jesse's speech.

  b. He thought that the bucket would fall on Jesse's head, knocking Jesse out.

  c. He stole Jesse's plan for giving cherry-flavored juice to everyone in the audience.

7. How did Daniel's trick go wrong?

  a. He did not position the bucket over the stage correctly.

  b. The bucket of red juice spilled early.

  c. Ms. Layton caught him with the bucket.

8. Which words help you to infer that Daniel's victims enjoyed seeing Daniel get embarrassed?

  a. *momentarily stunned*

  b. *laughing harder than everyone else*

  c. *target of his own prank*

9. What inference can you make based on what Ms. Layton says to Daniel?

  a. She meant to cause the bucket to tip and spill on Daniel.

  b. She thinks that Daniel meant to spill the punch on himself.

  c. She knows that Daniel has pulled many practical jokes before.

10. What can you infer about why the cherry drink incident changed Daniel?

  a. It made him lose his sense of humor and become angry.

  b. It made him appreciate what good friends his former victims were.

  c. It made him see that practical jokes aren't fun for the victim.

Mid-Unit Assessment • Unit 6 continued

Part 3 Fluency

Read the following passage once. Then read it again as your teacher times you. Underline the word you are reading when your teacher says to stop. Then answer the question.

"This was the most embarrassing day I've ever had," I told my
family, as we got ready for dinner. "I wish I could just start over."

Grandma sat at the dining room table listening to my tragic tale,
while Mom and Dave cooked dinner and made sympathetic noises.
Johnny, my brother, helped me set the table even though it wasn't his
turn. Who better to complain to than those who must love you no
matter what?

Finally, I got to the audition disaster. "You should have seen me
up on that stage, trying to keep my hair out of my face and my right
shoe from flying away. I showed them some moves from my modified
routine and wasn't surprised when they all started laughing."

"Renee and Joey were no help," I announced. I imitated Joey
singing my song and Renee's breaking my shoelace. Soon, I had
my family falling apart with laughter.

"Kelly," Mom giggled, "you're such a good mimic, so imaginative,
that I can picture it all just as you tell it."

"She's a good actress, too," Dave put in. "I still say your day
turned out well. You persisted through all of those problems, and
I'm proud of you."

Which of the following can you infer about Kelly's family?
a. They happily share their feelings and like to help each other.
b. They are too busy with their own interests to spend time together.
c. They enjoy making fun of each other when something goes wrong.

End-of-Unit Assessment
Unit 6

Part 1 Vocabulary

Circle *a* or *b* to answer each question.

WORD LIST

absurd
anguish
arise
concede
consequence
considerable
dismal
dramatic
escort
frustrated
misfortune
ominous
ordeal
petrify
treacherous
unfortunately

1. Is a rainbow usually an *ominous* sign?

    a. yes   **b.** no

2. Does an usher *escort* you to your seat at a theater?

    a. yes   **b.** no

3. If a person is in *anguish*, is he happy?

    a. yes   **b.** no

4. Does a disaster cause *considerable* damage?

    a. yes   **b.** no

Circle the letter of the word that best completes each sentence.

5. Rainy days are gloomy and _____.

    a. dismal   **b.** absurd   **c.** ordeal

6. The puppy grew _____ when it could not get the ball out from under the sofa.

    a. concede   **b.** arise   **c.** frustrated

7. The _____ announcement stunned the crowd.

    a. dramatic   **b.** misfortune   **c.** ordeal

8. Joe spoke quickly without thinking about negative _____.

    a. frustrated   **b.** escort   **c.** consequences

9. It was the town's _____ to have three floods in one year.

    a. misfortune   **b.** dismal   **c.** arise

End-of-Unit Assessment • Unit 6 continued

10. Strange noises in the night _____ my little sister.

    a. petrify   **b.** frustrated   **c.** anguish

11. Getting caught in traffic when she was in a hurry was an _____ for Kana.

    a. ordeal   **b.** arise   **c.** absurd

Circle the letter of the word that means the opposite of the underlined word.

12. It is <u>safe</u> to walk on an icy sidewalk.

    a. dramatic   **b.** dismal   **c.** treacherous

13. The clumsy actions of the clown were <u>sensible</u>.

    a. absurd   **b.** concede   **c.** ominous

Circle the letter of the word that correctly completes each sentence.

14. *Happy* is to *unhappy* as *fortunately* is to _____.

    a. frustrated   **b.** dismal   **c.** unfortunately

15. *Nap* is to *sleep* as *give up* is to _____.

    a. concede   **b.** arise   **c.** petrify

End-of-Unit Assessment • Unit 6 continued

Part 2 Comprehension: Inferencing
Read the passage and answer the questions at the
end of the passage.

Success Is No Mistake

What do you get when you mix talent, courage, and
hundreds of on-air mistakes? You get baseball personality
Jerry Coleman!   1

Jerry Coleman has been involved in baseball for most
of his 80 years. He has been a player, a coach, and a radio
announcer. He has entertained fans with great plays and
great broadcasting. He has also amused them with plenty
of embarrassing mix-ups.   2

An Awesome Career

Baseball has been a huge part of Coleman's life, but he
believes his military service was even more important.
Coleman served in World War II and the Korean War. He
was the only major league player ever to see combat in two
wars. As a fighter pilot, Coleman flew many missions in
treacherous territory. He was awarded a number of honors
for his bravery. His medals include 2 Distinguished Flying
Crosses and 13 Air Medals. He also received 3 Navy
Citations.   3

Between World War II and the Korean War, Coleman
played second base for the New York Yankees. He was a
player of considerable talent. During his career, he was
named Rookie of the Year, American League All-Star, *and*
Most Valuable Player in a World Series. The Yankees won
the World Series four times while he was on the team.   4

Coleman later worked one year as a Yankee's coach but
soon learned that he was better suited to radio work. He
announced the Yankees games for several years. Then, in
1972, Coleman became the announcer for the San Diego
Padres. He has filled that role for 32 seasons and is now
known as the voice of the San Diego Padres. He is a
talented announcer and popular with fans, athletes, and
fellow announcers.   5

End-of-Unit Assessment • Unit 6 continued

Coleman's Baseball Blunders

Coleman's talent is not the only thing he is famous for. **6** Anytime people talk about Jerry Coleman, they can't help mentioning his famous on-air mistakes. Coleman is known for mixing up expressions, words, and ideas in a way that can be very funny.

Some of Coleman's best-known mix-ups combine two **7** different expressions. For example, Coleman once meant to say that a player was throwing the ball, or warming up, in the bullpen. He combined the two ideas and said, "Rich Folkers is throwing up in the bullpen." Fans knew what he meant, but they got a big kick out of his mistake. Another time, Coleman mixed up the saying that "there are two sides to every story" with the expression "a flip of the coin." He got quite a laugh from the crowd when he put them together to say, "There are two heads to every coin."

Some of Coleman's mistakes happen when he mixes **8** up numbers. Can you catch the math errors in the following quotes?

"That's Hendrick's nineteenth homerun. One more and he reaches double figures."

"Montreal leads Atlanta by three, 5 to 1."

"Last night's homer was Willie Stargell's 399th career home run, leaving him one shy of 500."

"The new Haitian baseball can't weigh more than 4 ounces or less than 5."

Coleman also has a way of combining two ideas that **9** can't both be true. He once called a player a "right-handed southpaw." A "southpaw" is a left-handed baseball player, so Coleman left fans wondering whether the player was right- or left-handed. On another occasion he announced, "They throw Winfield out at second, and he's safe." A player who is thrown out isn't safe—so what happened to Winfield? During one broadcast, listening fans didn't know whether the player was up or down when Coleman described the action in the following way: "He leaped up to make one of those diving stops only he can make."

End-of-Unit Assessment • Unit 6 continued

Perhaps the funniest of Coleman's quotes are those that create a crazy picture. For example, here's his description of a player missing a catch: "Winfield goes back to the wall, he hits his head on the wall, and it rolls off! It's rolling all the way back to second base. This is a terrible thing for the Padres." Of course, it was the ball that was rolling, not the player's head. That comment had all of Coleman's listeners rolling with laughter.

10

A Favorite With the Fans

In 2005, Coleman was honored for his work as a radio announcer by the Baseball Hall of Fame. How can a man who makes so many mistakes earn such an honor? For one thing, Coleman's blunders make him a favorite with fans. His mistakes add to the fun of listening to his broadcasts. Although he makes blunders, Coleman's mistakes are rarely misleading. Fans know what he means to say and get a laugh out of his funny mix-ups. Fans may like him even more because he's a celebrity who makes mistakes that any of us could make.

11

How does Coleman feel about his blunders? He enjoys his job and doesn't take his mistakes too seriously. In fact, he was once quoted as saying, "I've made a couple of mistakes I'd like to do over." Well, you know what he meant.

12

Circle the letter of the correct answer to each question.

1. Which best describes Jerry Coleman?

   a. He is a regular guy, but he is confused by the rules of baseball.

   b. He is a baseball expert, but he sometimes mixes up words.

   c. He is a great player, but he does a poor job of announcing baseball.

End-of-Unit Assessment • Unit 6 continued

2. According to paragraph 3, which inference can you make about what Coleman believes?

   a. An athlete's job is more important than a coach's job.

   b. A coach's job is more important than an announcer's job.

   c. A soldier's job is more important than an athlete's job.

3. Why do Coleman's listeners laugh at what he says?

   a. They like the way he makes mistakes on purpose to get a laugh.

   b. They like him but think he mixes up words in a funny way.

   c. They think he's a fool who doesn't know what he's talking about.

4. Based on the text, what inference can you make about Coleman's time as a coach?

   a. His salary was too low for such a skilled coach.

   b. His players laughed whenever he made mistakes, so he quit.

   c. He realized that he wasn't a very good coach.

5. Which job did Coleman have between World War II and the Korean War?

   a. major league second baseman

   b. major league coach

   c. radio announcer

6. Why did the crowd laugh when Coleman said "There are two heads to every coin"?

   a. What he said was funny but true.

   b. There is only one head on a coin.

   c. He meant to say that there are two tails to every coin.

End-of-Unit Assessment • Unit 6 continued

7. What inference can you make about the **effect** of Coleman's math errors?

   a. The audience can figure out what he means and still get a laugh.

   b. His math errors affect the scores of the games he is announcing.

   c. His math errors caused Coleman to lose his job as a coach.

8. Which prediction can you make based on Jerry Coleman's career?

   a. Other announcers will make intentional mistakes so they can get into the Hall of Fame.

   b. Coleman will be remembered for his funny mistakes as much as for his achievements.

   c. In the future, radio stations will avoid hiring announcers who mix up their words.

9. Which of the following is a **fact** stated by the author in paragraph 11?

   a. *In 2005, Coleman was honored for his work as a radio announcer by the Baseball Hall of Fame.*

   b. *Fans may like him even more because he's a celebrity who makes mistakes that any of us could make.*

   c. *Coleman's blunders make him a favorite with fans.*

10. What can you infer about what Coleman meant when he said, "I've made a couple of mistakes I'd like to do over."?

   a. He would like to go back and do some things differently.

   b. He likes to remember the funny things he's said.

   c. He wants to repeat his blunders on purpose to get laughs.

End-of-Unit Assessment • Unit 6 continued

Part 3 Fluency

Read the following passage once. Then read it again as your teacher times you. Underline the word you are reading when your teacher says to stop. Then answer the question.

Dan Quayle was the vice president under President George H. W. Bush from 1989 to 1993. He was 41 when he became vice president. On June 15, 1992, the vice president attended a spelling bee at the Luis Munoz Rivera School in Trenton, New Jersey. Reporters were there, too, with television cameras to record the visit. Vice President Quayle asked 12-year-old William Figueroa to spell the word *potato*. The sixth-grader walked to the chalkboard and wrote *p-o-t-a-t-o*. The vice president told Figueroa that he had made a mistake and asked him to add an *e* on the end of the word.

"I knew he was wrong," Figueroa later told comedian David Letterman. "But since he's the vice president, I went back and put an *e* on ([it]) and went back to my seat." Unfortunately for Vice President Quayle, it turned out that Figueroa was the one who was right. The word *potato* doesn't have an *e* on the end.

Vice President Quayle conceded he had made a spelling error, but he said the flashcard he was holding at the spelling bee had the word *potato* misspelled. Still, Quayle suffered dire consequences. His political career was never quite the same afterward.

Why do you think William Figueroa listened to the vice president?

a. He thought that the vice president was correct, so he changed the spelling.

b. He respected the vice president and didn't want to correct him.

c. He thought it would be funny to make a mistake in front of the cameras.

Mid-Unit Assessment
Unit 7

Part 1 Vocabulary

Circle *a* or *b* to answer each question.

1. Can a *colleague* also be a friend?

   a. yes   **b.** no

2. Does a *legendary* site such as the Alamo have a lot of stories told about it?

   a. yes   **b.** no

3. If Marie is *determined* to become a doctor, will she give up on her goal easily?

   a. yes   **b.** no

4. If an announcement is *widespread*, is it a secret?

   a. yes   **b.** no

5. If your friend is *recognizable* in a crowd, do you have a hard time finding her?

   a. yes   **b.** no

Circle the letter of the word that best completes each sentence.

6. The cafe became such a _____ success that the owner was able to open another one.

   a. trend   **b.** financial   **c.** determined

7. I _____ Luke as my best friend.

   a. fulfill   **b.** defy   **c.** regard

8. Today's _____ of the newspaper has an interesting story about Alaska.

   a. edition   **b.** candidate   **c.** attempt

WORD LIST

attempt

candidate

colleague

defy

determined

edition

expectation

facilities

financial

fulfill

legendary

recognizable

regard

thoroughly

trend

widespread

Mid-Unit Assessment • Unit 7 continued

9. The _____ at the gym are great for holding our gymnastics classes.

    a. facilities   **b.** regard   **c.** colleagues

10. The _____ for mayor promised to change how the city handles collecting garbage.

    a. candidate   **b.** trend   **c.** attempt

11. Jason got his hair cut in the style that is the latest _____.

    a. attempt   **b.** edition   **c.** trend

12. Miko scraped the bowl _____ until every bit was gone.

    a. thoroughly   **b.** fulfilled   **c.** financial

13. Janna's parents have the _____ that she will go to college after high school.

    a. candidate   **b.** trend   **c.** expectation

Circle the letter of the form of the word that correctly completes each sentence.

14. Adam tried to _____ the team rules by always showing up late for practice.

    a. defiance   **b.** defy   **c.** defiantly

15. A _____ job makes you happy to go to work each day.

    a. fulfill   **b.** fulfillment   **c.** fulfilling

Mid-Unit Assessment • Unit 7 continued

Part 2 Comprehension: Metacognition

Read the passage and answer the questions at the end of
the passage.

The Edsel

New car models come out every year. Many people can't 1
wait to see how styles of cars change from previous years.
They also want to know what the new trends are. Are new
cars safer? Do they use less gas? Are they small and
sporty or long and sleek? What are the new colors?
Carmakers spend a lot of time and money making sure that
their cars give people what they want. After all, a car is a
huge financial investment for most people. Customers can
be very demanding when they have to pay a lot of money
for a new car.

The Ford Motor Company learned an important lesson in 2
1957 when it made a car that few people wanted. The
company thought that this car would be a real winner. In
fact, the expectation for this car was so great that it took a
year of research just to name it. Management wanted a
name that would set the car apart from other cars. More
than 2,000 names were considered. Then people who
worked for the company were asked for their suggestions.
About 8,000 additional names were received! Even a
famous poet was asked to suggest names. The poet came
up with silly names such as Utopian Turtletop. No one
could agree on a name, so the company chairman, Henry
Ford II, finally said, "Why don't we just call it 'Edsel'?"

Edsel was a Ford family name. Henry Ford had begun 3
the Ford Motor Company in 1903, and *Edsel* was the name
of his only son. Edsel Ford had died in 1943, and his son,
Henry Ford II, was now chairman of the company. The name
didn't mean anything to anyone outside the Ford family. Yet
the name stuck, and the Edsel was born.

Mid-Unit Assessment • Unit 7 continued

Edsel's Design

The Edsel was designed to appeal to young businessmen. It was to look expensive but have a medium price. The first few designs for the car had to be changed to make the car practical. The final design was a disappointment. Some people said the front end looked like a car sucking a lemon. Other critics said that it looked like a horse collar.

4

Actually, the specifications for the first Edsel weren't very different from other Ford models. It was built in a similar way to other Ford cars. In fact, it used parts from different Ford models. At Ford manufacturing plants, every sixty-first car on the assembly line was an Edsel. Workers attached parts originally designed for other Ford cars onto the Edsel. However, building the Edsel from parts of other Ford cars was complicated. Many mistakes were made in building those first cars.

5

Bad Marketing

To get the word out about the new car, 75 writers for car magazines were asked to test-drive the new Edsels. The 75 cars were tested by Ford for two months before they were handed over to the writers for their test-drives. Unfortunately, only 68 cars could be driven. Parts from the remaining seven cars had to be used to fix problems with the other cars.

6

The 68 cars didn't do very well during their test-drives with the writers. The cars needed repairs after the test-drives. The average repair bill was $10,000. This amount was more than twice the price of the most expensive Edsel model! You can imagine that the car magazine writers didn't have very good things to say about the Edsel.

7

Introducing the Edsel

The Edsel was introduced anyway in 1957 when ads announced, "There has never been a car like the Edsel." This bold statement was widespread. In the first week, nearly 3 million people visited car dealers, but few people bought an Edsel.

8

Mid-Unit Assessment • Unit 7 continued

In another attempt to generate interest in the Edsel, Ford sponsored a one-hour TV special called *The Edsel Show*. Big-time singers performed, and the ratings were huge. Edsel commercials also ran during the popular TV show *Wagon Train*, but people still didn't buy the cars. **9**

A big part of the problem was that in 1957, car sales in general didn't meet expectations. Before 1957, there had been a boom in car sales. Cars had become more than just a form of transportation—they had become a symbol of how well people were doing. In the early 1950s, many new models of cars came out. By 1957, however, carmakers such as DeSoto, Mercury, and Dodge sold only about half the number of cars they had sold in 1956. In its first year, about 63,000 Edsels were sold. The Ford Motor Company had expected to sell 200,000. **10**

Two other facts hurt the Edsel. In 1956, Ford had introduced the Ford Fairlane. People liked it better than the Edsel, especially because it cost less. Then in 1957, the American Motors Company came out with the Rambler. People liked that car better than the Edsel, too. **11**

The End of the Edsel

Ford made a 1959 model of the Edsel. They changed the design and marketing, but the changes weren't enough. Fewer than 45,000 Edsels were sold. In 1960, Ford tried to make the Edsel look more glamorous, but it was too late. The Edsel was doomed. In that year, less than 3,000 Edsels were sold. It was the last year that the Edsel was made. **12**

Ford learned some crucial lessons from the Edsel failure. It learned that it doesn't matter how big a company is or how much marketing it has done. No company can tell people what they want. People decide what they want, and companies must meet their customers' demands if they want to stay in business. Ford also learned not to build up a new car too much in people's minds before they see it. The real thing, like the Edsel, might not meet expectations. **13**

Mid-Unit Assessment • Unit 7 continued

Circle the letter of the correct answer to each question.

1. What is an important thing to do before you read a passage such as "The Edsel"?

   a. Count the number of paragraphs to see how long it will take to read the passage.

   b. Preview the title and subheads, and set a goal for reading.

   c. Look for important names and dates in order to make a graphic organizer.

2. Which of the following did the Ford Motor Company do in 1957?

   a. The company built a car that few people wanted.

   b. The company built a car that people wanted to pay more money for.

   c. The company built a car named after a famous poet.

3. Which of the following can best help prepare you to summarize a passage like "The Edsel"?

   a. Preview and make a prediction.

   b. Ask a "between the lines" question.

   c. Identify the topic and the main idea.

4. Where did the name *Edsel* come from?

   a. *Edsel* was the name that researchers suggested.

   b. *Edsel* was the name of Henry Ford's son.

   c. *Edsel* was an idea that a famous poet came up with.

5. Which of the following is a good question to ask to help you understand the passage?

   a. Who were the writers who did the test-drives?

   b. Why was the Edsel a failure?

   c. What year did the Edsel come on the market?

6. Which was probably the worst marketing idea for introducing the Edsel?

  a. hosting a one-hour TV special called *The Edsel Show*

  b. running commercials during the TV show *Wagon Train*

  c. having car magazine writers test-drive new Edsels

7. How does making a prediction help you understand a passage such as "The Edsel"?

  a. Making a prediction helps me carefully read the passage to see if the prediction is correct.

  b. Making a prediction helps me gather details and important information to write a summary.

  c. Making a prediction helps me visualize what is happening in the passage.

8. Which of the following would help you understand the passage?

  a. thinking about how the passage relates to something I already know

  b. thinking about why Henry Ford named his only son Edsel

  c. thinking about why some cars use less gasoline than others

9. What crucial lesson did Ford learn from the Edsel?

  a. Never name a car after a family member.

  b. Companies must meet customers' demands.

  c. Marketing a product on television is useless.

10. How does choosing the strategy of questioning help you understand a passage such as "The Edsel"?

  a. Questioning helps me read the passage faster and skip the unimportant details.

  b. Questioning helps me identify and think about important ideas in the passage.

  c. Questioning helps me read the passage once and understand all the ideas in it.

Mid-Unit Assessment • Unit 7 continued

Part 3 Fluency

Read the following passage once. Then read it again as your teacher times you. Underline the word you are reading when your teacher says to stop. Then answer the question.

On a clear night in 1877, an Italian astronomer named Giovanni Schiaparelli looked at Mars through his telescope and thought he saw a network of straight lines. He called the lines *canali*, which means "channels" in Italian. In English, his discovery was mistakenly translated as "canals."

Schiaparelli's discovery caused great excitement. Many people began to regard the canals as proof of life on Mars. The American astronomer Percival Lowell claimed that the canals were irrigation ditches dug by intelligent beings. Lowell suggested that the canals carried water from the polar ice caps of Mars to populated areas. His views sparked a trend toward believing in life on Mars.

Other astronomers disagreed with Lowell. In 1903, two Americans claimed the canals were really an optical illusion, or a visual image that is misleading. The debate was finally settled in the 1960s, when NASA sent the *Mariner* spacecraft to Mars. Photographs from the *Mariner* proved beyond a doubt that there were no canals on Mars. The barren landscape of Mars is dotted with craters, not lined with irrigation ditches.

How would summarizing help you understand this passage?

a. It would help me remember the steps that scientists took to build a spacecraft to explore Mars.

b. It would help me understand why a theory about Mars was proposed and then disproved.

c. It would help me predict that scientists have not found water anywhere else in the galaxy.

Name _____ Date _____

End-of-Unit Assessment
Unit 7

Part 1 Vocabulary

Circle *a* or *b* to answer each question.

WORD LIST

- aerial
- celestial
- commonplace
- descriptive
- gradual
- humankind
- illustrate
- insight
- invasion
- lesser
- minority
- mislead
- multitude
- placid
- profound
- utmost

1. Is a grain of sand *commonplace* on a beach?

    a. yes   **b.** no

2. Does it take a *multitude* of people to fill a stadium?

    a. yes   **b.** no

3. Would you look down to see something that is *celestial*?

    a. yes   **b.** no

4. Does *humankind* include children and teenagers?

    a. yes   **b.** no

5. If there are four cats and three dogs, are the cats the *minority*?

    a. yes   **b.** no

Circle the letter of the word that best completes each sentence.

6. Shawna didn't mean to _____ people, but they believed that her fiction story was true.

    a. placid   **b.** illustrate   **c.** mislead

7. The author's _____ text made it easy to visualize the farm.

    a. descriptive   **b.** utmost   **c.** aerial

8. Jack's _____ speech about the need to care for all people made us think deeply.

    a. profound   **b.** invasion   **c.** lesser

End-of-Unit Assessment • Unit 7 continued

9. Dana didn't notice the change in Eli's height because it was so _____.

   a. aerial   **b.** gradual   **c.** celestial

10. The _____ of the bees made us run for cover.

   a. insight   **b.** lesser   **c.** invasion

11. Winnie wants to _____ the story using bright-colored crayons.

   a. mislead   **b.** illustrate   **c.** profound

12. Tanya's _____ into the problem helped us solve it right away.

   a. insight   **b.** invasion   **c.** lesser

13. The lake is very _____ on a calm summer day.

   a. celestial   **b.** placid   **c.** descriptive

14. It was exciting to watch the airplanes do tricks during the _____ show.

   a. aerial   **b.** invasion   **c.** profound

15. James gave his _____ effort to move the rock, but it was too heavy.

   a. lesser   **b.** utmost   **c.** humankind

End-of-Unit Assessment • Unit 7 continued

Part 2 Comprehension: Metacognition

Read the passage and answer the questions at the end of
the passage.

April Fools' Day

Have you ever been tricked on April Fools' Day? Have   1
you ever tried to trick someone on the first day of April?
Some people can't wait for April Fools' Day. They plan their
tricks weeks ahead of time. On the other hand, this holiday
annoys many people. Having tricks and jokes played on
them does not amuse them at all.

No one is certain how April Fools' Day began. One   2
assumption is that it relates to the start of spring. Nature
fools us with a few nice, warm days, but then it throws in
cold, gloomy days. Another idea is that April Fools' Day is
related to games that were played during end-of-winter
celebrations in ancient Rome. The most widespread
explanation, though, is that it has to do with a change in
the calendar.

A History of Fools

Before 1582, Europeans used a calendar in which the   3
New Year began on March 25. Because that date fell during
a religious week, many people celebrated the New Year on
April 1 instead. Then another calendar was adopted in
1582. New Year's Day was moved to January 1. Because
news spread slowly, some people in France didn't know
about the change in the calendar. Maybe some people just
didn't accept the change. Whatever the reason, their friends
began to play tricks on them. The first tricks involved a visit
on April 1 to wish friends a happy New Year, even though it
wasn't the New Year. Another trick involved sending
someone an invitation to a New Year's party. When that
person arrived at the location, he or she would discover
that there was no party.

French and English colonists probably brought April **4**
Fools' Day to the Americas during the 1700s. A person
fooled on April 1 became known as an April fool. In France
an April fool is called an "April fish" or "young fish." A
young fish is easy to catch.

In Scotland, an April fool is called an April "gowk." *Gowk* **5**
is the Scottish word for "cuckoo." Some people think that
cuckoo birds look or sound silly. As a result, these birds are
a symbol for someone who can be easily tricked. April Fools'
is celebrated for two days in Scotland. The second day is
called "Taily Day." Tricks on this day involve the back of the
body. Taily Day is responsible for the popularity of the "kick
me" sign taped to someone's back.

Different parts of England have different words for an **6**
April fool. In some places, the person is called an April
"noddy" or an April "guckaw" or "gawk" (also words for
cuckoo). Elsewhere in England, an April fool is called an
April "gawby," "gobby," or "gob." "Tailpipe Day" is also
celebrated in parts of England. In the United States, the
day is simply called April Fools' Day.

Pranks, Hoaxes, and Tricks

To be thoroughly correct, April Fools' Day tricks should **7**
be played before noon. The victim of a joke played after
noon has the right to shout, "April Fools' gone past, and
you're the biggest fool at last!" The only other rule is that
tricks should not harm anyone.

Some old tricks included sending a child to a store for **8**
items that did not exist, such as "elbow grease." Children,
on the other hand, tricked their parents by replacing the
sugar in the sugar bowl with salt or by setting the clocks
back an hour.

Many April Fools' tricks are played through the media. **9**
In 1949, a radio disc jockey in New Zealand warned his
listeners that a swarm of wasps was headed their way. He
told people to pull their socks over their pants legs as they
left their homes. He also misled his listeners by telling
them to smear honey outside their houses to keep the

wasps away. The New Zealand Broadcasting Service did not think the hoax was funny. Now every year a memo is sent out before April 1 reminding New Zealand radio stations that their job is to report the truth.

In 1984, an Illinois newspaper played an April Fools' Day hoax. The newspaper announced a contest to see who could save the most daylight for Daylight Saving Time. People were told to put out jars to catch daylight. The rules were that only pure daylight could be saved. No light from dawn or dusk was allowed. No moonlight was allowed either. The contest generated a huge response. The newspaper received national attention for the silly contest. 10

On the same day in Orlando, Florida, another newspaper described a new type of pet. The pet was called a Tasmanian mock walrus, or TMW for short. It looked like a walrus, but it was only four inches long. The newspaper said that the TMW was a wonderful pet. It purred like a cat and used a litter box. It acted calm like a hamster. It never needed a bath. The best part was that it ate cockroaches. The TMW could rid a house of a cockroach invasion. The paper said that the local pest control people were trying to keep TMWs from becoming pets because they would ruin the pest control business. The newspaper received a multitude of calls from readers wanting to know how they could get a TMW. 11

Yet another April Fool's joke was played in 1993. A German radio station announced that joggers running through a park could not exceed a speed of six miles per hour. The squirrels in the park were busy building nests. The radio announcer told listeners that joggers who went faster than that speed would disturb the squirrels. 12

Knowing that April 1 is a historically special day should keep you on your toes. If you're not careful, you may become known as an April gowk or April noddy! 13

End-of-Unit Assessment • Unit 7 continued

Circle the letter of the correct answer to each question.

1. Two kinds of people are mentioned in the passage. Which kind is NOT mentioned?

   a. people who plan tricks for April Fools' Day

   b. people who protest against April Fools' Day

   c. people who do not like being tricked on April Fools' Day

2. Which is the most widespread explanation of how April Fools' Day began?

   a. Its beginning is related to the start of spring.

   b. Its beginning is related to games that were played during the ancient Romans' end-of-winter celebration.

   c. Its beginning is related to a change in the calendar.

3. Why would thinking about text structure help you understand this passage?

   a. It would help me organize the information and understand it better.

   b. It would help me visualize every fact and detail to understand the text better.

   c. It would help me summarize the main idea and all the important details.

4. Why would thinking about making inferences help a reader understand this passage?

   a. It could lead to inventing new kinds of jokes and hoaxes to play on April Fools' Day.

   b. It could make a reader consider how people feel about April Fools' Day.

   c. It could help a reader understand who invented the calendar.

5. Which image would you visualize in paragraph 5?

   a. the country of Scotland

   b. a "kick me" sign taped to someone's back

   c. a "kick me" sign taped to a cuckoo bird

End-of-Unit Assessment • Unit 7 continued

6. Why would a graphic organizer be helpful in understanding the section "Pranks, Hoaxes, and Tricks"?

   a. A graphic organizer could be used to organize the different tricks played on April Fools' Day.

   b. A graphic organizer could be used to predict what other kinds of tricks the media will play on its audience.

   c. A graphic organizer could be used to help preview the important details in the passage.

7. Why do you think the media play April Fools' Day tricks?

   a. They can reach many people with one trick.

   b. People who work for the media are known to play tricks.

   c. The media always follow traditional customs.

8. Which strategy best helps you to understand the hoax played by the Illinois newspaper?

   a. predicting, because it helps to know what will happen next and who caught the most daylight in a jar

   b. inferencing, because I think more deeply about the purpose of Daylight Saving Time

   c. visualizing, because picturing helps me understand how silly the idea was

9. Why did so many people respond to the article about the TMW pet?

   a. They were mad that the newspaper was playing a joke on its readers.

   b. The description made the TMW sound lovable and useful.

   c. They wanted to enter a contest to win the TMW.

10. How does knowing which strategies to use help you better understand a passage?

   a. Knowing which strategies to use helps me understand that passages always contain incorrect information.

   b. Knowing which strategies to use helps me focus on the important details and remember them.

   c. Knowing which strategies to use helps me identify all the unimportant details.

End-of-Unit Assessment • Unit 7 continued

Part 3 Fluency

Read the following passage once. Then read it again as your teacher times you. Underline the word you are reading when your teacher says to stop. Then answer the question.

Try to picture what you or your family members might have done upon hearing that Martians had landed. As people listened to the radio broadcast of *The War of the Worlds*, many panicked. They mistakenly believed that the play was a news broadcast, and their fear caused them to act without thinking.

Many people took action. They packed blankets and supplies in their cars and left their towns. Some people called police stations, newspapers, and radio stations. They asked for advice about how to protect themselves. Others were concerned about the persons they cared about. They called their friends and family members to warn them of the danger. Some drove to the homes of family members so that they could be together.

Clearly, voices of knowledgeable people commenting on the invasion made the situation especially believable. Many listeners probably felt like the one who said, "I knew it had to be an awfully dangerous situation when all those military men were there."

The realistic nature of the broadcast may have fired up listeners' imaginations. They may have imagined things that did not really exist.

If you did not understand this passage, what should you do?

a. Stop reading and think about choosing strategies that would help me understand the passage.

b. Use all six strategies before I read, as I read, and after I read the passage.

c. Keep reading the passage aloud until I understand it.

Individual Assessment Record

Name _____   Class _____

Informal Reading Inventory						
Date administered	Missed words	Misread words	Added words	Comprehension items answered incorrectly	Total number of incorrect items	Final score

	Mid-Unit Assessment				End-of-Unit Assessment				Average Unit scores			
Student Guide Unit	Vocabulary	Comprehension	Fluency	Total Score	Vocabulary	Comprehension	Fluency	Total Score	Vocabulary	Comprehension	Fluency	Total Score
Unit 1 Summarizing												
Unit 2 Questioning												
Unit 3 Predicting												
Unit 4 Text Structure												
Unit 5 Visualizing												
Unit 6 Inferencing												
Unit 7 Metacognition												

Fluency Word Count													
Unit 1 Assessment		Unit 2 Assessment		Unit 3 Assessment		Unit 4 Assessment		Unit 5 Assessment		Unit 6 Assessment		Unit 7 Assessment	
Mid-Unit	End-of-Unit	Mid-Unit	End-of-Unit	Mid-Unit	End-of-Unit	Mid-Unit	End-of-Unit	Mid-Unit	End-of-Unit	Mid-Unit	End-of-Unit	Mid-Unit	End-of-Unit

Class Assessment Record

Class _____

Student Name	Unit 1 Mid-Unit	Unit 1 End-of-Unit	Unit 2 Mid-Unit	Unit 2 End-of-Unit	Unit 3 Mid-Unit	Unit 3 End-of-Unit	Unit 4 Mid-Unit	Unit 4 End-of-Unit	Unit 5 Mid-Unit	Unit 5 End-of-Unit	Unit 6 Mid-Unit	Unit 6 End-of-Unit	Unit 7 Mid-Unit	Unit 7 End-of-Unit

Globe Fearon

 **READING SYSTEM**

CERTIFICATE OF ACHIEVEMENT

Awarded to

_____

for the successful completion of

_____

Teacher _____

Date _____   Class _____

Answer Key

Informal Reading Inventory Passage

1. c
2. c
3. a

UNIT 1 Summarizing

Mid-Unit Assessment
Part 1 Vocabulary

1. b	6. b	11. c
2. b	7. a	12. a
3. b	8. b	13. b
4. a	9. b	14. b
5. a	10. a	15. b

Part 2 Comprehension: Summarizing

1. a	5. b	8. a
2. b	6. c	9. b
3. a	7. b	10. b
4. b		

Part 3 Fluency
c

End-of-Unit Assessment
Part 1 Vocabulary

1. a	6. c	11. b
2. b	7. c	12. c
3. b	8. b	13. c
4. a	9. a	14. c
5. b	10. c	15. a

Part 2 Comprehension: Summarizing

1. c	5. b	8. a
2. a	6. b	9. b
3. c	7. a	10. b
4. b		

Part 3 Fluency
a

UNIT 2 Questioning

Mid-Unit Assessment
Part 1 Vocabulary

1. a	6. c	11. a
2. b	7. b	12. b
3. b	8. a	13. a
4. a	9. a	14. c
5. b	10. b	15. c

Part 2 Comprehension: Questioning

1. b	5. a	8. b
2. b	6. a	9. c
3. c	7. a	10. b
4. b		

Part 3 Fluency
b

End-of-Unit Assessment
Part 1 Vocabulary

1. a	6. a	11. c
2. b	7. c	12. a
3. b	8. c	13. b
4. a	9. c	14. c
5. a	10. a	15. b

Part 2 Comprehension: Questioning

1. a	5. b	8. b
2. b	6. a	9. b
3. a	7. c	10. b
4. c		

Part 3 Fluency
c

Unit 3 Predicting

Mid-Unit Assessment
Part 1 Vocabulary

1. b	6. a	11. b
2. a	7. c	12. c
3. a	8. a	13. b
4. b	9. c	14. a
5. b	10. c	15. a

Answer Key continued

Part 2 Comprehension: Predicting

1. c	5. b	8. c
2. a	6. a	9. a
3. a	7. b	10. b
4. c		

Part 3 Fluency
a

End-of-Unit Assessment
Part 1 Vocabulary

1. b	6. b	11. b
2. a	7. a	12. a
3. a	8. c	13. a
4. b	9. c	14. b
5. a	10. c	15. b

Part 2 Comprehension: Predicting

1. c	5. b	8. b
2. b	6. c	9. c
3. b	7. a	10. a
4. a		

Part 3 Fluency
b

Unit 4 Text Structure

Mid-Unit Assessment
Part 1 Vocabulary

1. b	6. b	11. a
2. a	7. c	12. a
3. b	8. b	13. b
4. b	9. c	14. b
5. a	10. a	15. b

Part 2 Comprehension: Text Structure

1. b	5. c	8. b
2. b	6. a	9. c
3. a	7. c	10. b
4. a		

Part 3 Fluency
c

End-of-Unit Assessment
Part 1 Vocabulary

1. a	6. b	11. a
2. b	7. a	12. c
3. a	8. c	13. c
4. a	9. a	14. a
5. a	10. b	15. c

Part 2 Comprehension: Text Structure

1. c	5. a	8. a
2. b	6. c	9. b
3. b	7. a	10. a
4. a		

Part 3 Fluency
c

Unit 5 Visualizing

Mid-Unit Assessment
Part 1 Vocabulary

1. a	6. c	11. c
2. a	7. b	12. b
3. b	8. a	13. a
4. a	9. c	14. a
5. b	10. c	15. b

Part 2 Comprehension: Visualizing

1. a	5. c	8. b
2. b	6. a	9. c
3. a	7. c	10. b
4. c		

Part 3 Fluency
b

End-of-Unit Assessment
Part 1 Vocabulary

1. a	6. b	11. c
2. b	7. b	12. c
3. a	8. c	13. b
4. b	9. b	14. a
5. a	10. a	15. c

Answer Key continued

Part 2 Comprehension: Visualizing

1. a	5. b	8. c
2. b	6. a	9. c
3. a	7. b	10. a
4. b		

Part 3 Fluency
a

Unit 6 Inferencing

Mid-Unit Assessment
Part 1 Vocabulary

1. a	6. c	11. a
2. a	7. c	12. b
3. b	8. a	13. a
4. a	9. a	14. c
5. a	10. b	15. a

Part 2 Comprehension: Inferencing

1. b	5. c	8. b
2. a	6. a	9. c
3. b	7. b	10. c
4. b		

Part 3 Fluency
a

End-of-Unit Assessment
Part 1 Vocabulary

1. b	6. c	11. a
2. a	7. a	12. c
3. b	8. c	13. a
4. a	9. a	14. c
5. a	10. a	15. a

Part 2 Comprehension: Inferencing

1. b	5. a	8. b
2. c	6. b	9. a
3. b	7. a	10. a
4. c		

Part 3 Fluency
b

Unit 7 Metacognition

Mid-Unit Assessment
Part 1 Vocabulary

1. a	6. b	11. c
2. a	7. c	12. a
3. b	8. a	13. c
4. b	9. a	14. b
5. b	10. a	15. c

Part 2 Comprehension: Metacognition

1. b	5. b	8. a
2. a	6. c	9. b
3. c	7. a	10. b
4. b		

Part 3 Fluency
b

End-of-Unit Assessment
Part 1 Vocabulary

1. a	6. c	11. b
2. a	7. a	12. a
3. b	8. a	13. b
4. a	9. b	14. a
5. b	10. c	15. b

Part 2 Comprehension: Metacognition

1. b	5. b	8. c
2. c	6. a	9. b
3. a	7. a	10. b
4. b		

Part 3 Fluency
a